Mixed Breed Cats

Our Best Friends

The Beagle	The Labrador Retriever
The Boxer	Lizards
The Bulldog	The Miniature Schnauzer
Caring for Your Mutt	Mixed Breed Cats
The Dachshund	The Poodle
Ferrets	The Pug
Fetch this Book	Rabbits
Gerbils	The Rottweiler
The German Shepherd	The Shih Tzu
The Golden Retriever	Snakes
Guinea Pigs	Turtles
Hamsters	The Yorkshire Terrier

OUR BEST FRIENDS

Mixed Breed Cats

Janice Biniok

ELDORADO INK

Produced by OTTN Publishing, Stockton, New Jersey

Eldorado Ink
PO Box 100097
Pittsburgh, PA 15233
www.eldoradoink.com

CPSIA compliance information: Batch#101909-6. For further information, contact
Eldorado Ink at info@eldoradoink.com.

First printing

1 3 5 7 9 8 6 4 2

Library of Congress Cataloging-in-Publication Data

   Biniok, Janice.
    Mixed breed cats / by Janice Biniok.
      p. cm. — (Our best friends)
    Includes bibliographical references and index.
    ISBN 978-1-932904-62-8
    1. Cats. I. Title.
    SF442.B56 2010
    636.8—dc22

                2009041443

Photo credits: Centers for Disease Control and Prevention, 78, 85; Paula Holzapfel, cover
image (bottom inset); Howcheng (http://commons.wikimedia.org/wiki/File:Cat_claw_close
up.jpg), 59; © iStockphoto.com/archives, 3; © iStockphoto.com/Lree, 63; Sarah Marriage
(http://www.flickr.com/photos/semarr/270169158), 31; Joel Mills (http://en.wikipedia.org/wiki
/File:Feline_identifying_microchip.jpg), 50; Courtesy National Association of Professional
Pet Sitters, 72; Marie-Lan Nguyen/Wikimedia Commons, 28; Used under license from
Shutterstock, Inc., 8, 10, 13, 15, 17, 18, 20, 21, 23, 24, 29, 32, 33, 35, 37, 38, 40, 42, 44,
45, 47, 48, 51, 53, 54, 56, 57, 58, 60, 65, 67, 69, 71, 73, 75, 76, 81, 82 (both), 86, 92, 94,
96, 97, 100, cover images (main image, top and middle inset) back cover; Frank Wouters
(http://flickr.com/photos/90901507@N00), 26.

**For information about custom editions, special sales, or premiums,
please contact our special sales department at info@eldoradoink.com.**

TABLE OF CONTENTS

Introduction

GARY KORSGAARD, DVM

The mutually beneficial relationship between humans and animals began long before the dawn of recorded history. Archaeologists believe that humans began to capture and tame wild goats, sheep, and pigs more than 9,000 years ago. These animals were then bred for specific purposes, such as providing humans with a reliable source of food or providing furs and hides that could be used for clothing or the construction of dwellings.

Other animals had been sought for companionship and assistance even earlier. The dog, believed to be the first animal domesticated, began living and working with Stone Age humans in Europe more than 14,000 years ago. Some archaeologists believe that wild dogs and humans were drawn together because both hunted the same prey. By taming and training dogs, humans became more effective hunters. Dogs, meanwhile, enjoyed the social contact with humans and benefited from greater access to food and warm shelter. Dogs soon became beloved pets as well as trusted workers. This can be seen from the many artifacts depicting dogs that have been found at ancient sites in Asia, Europe, North America, and the Middle East.

The earliest domestic cats appeared in the Middle East about 5,000 years ago. Small wild cats were probably first attracted to human settlements because plenty of rodents could be found wherever harvested grain was stored. Cats played a useful role in hunting and killing these pests, and it is likely that grateful humans rewarded them for this assistance. Over time, these small cats gave up some of their aggressive wild behaviors and began living among humans. Cats eventually became so popular in ancient Egypt that they were believed to possess magical powers. Cat statues were placed outside homes to ward off evil spirits, and mummified cats were included in royal tombs to accompany their owners into the afterlife.

Today, few people believe that cats have supernatural powers, but most pet owners feel a magical bond with their pets, whether they are dogs, cats, hamsters, rabbits, horses, or parrots. The lives of pets and their people become inextricably intertwined, providing strong emotional and physical rewards for both humans and animals. People of all ages can benefit from the loving companionship of a pet. Not surprisingly, then, pet ownership is widespread. Recent statistics indicate that about 60 percent of all households in the United States and Canada have at least one pet, while the figure is close to 50 percent of households in the United Kingdom. For millions of people, therefore, pets truly have become their "best friends."

Finding the best animal friend can be a challenge, however. Not only are there many types of domesticated pets, but each has specific needs, characteristics, and personality traits. Even within a category of pets, such as dogs, different breeds will flourish in different surroundings and with different treatment. For example, a German Shepherd may not be the right pet for a person living in a cramped urban apartment; that person might be better off caring for a smaller dog like a Toy Poodle or Shih Tzu, or perhaps a cat. On the other hand, an active person who loves the outdoors may prefer the companionship of a Labrador Retriever to that of a small dog or a passive indoor pet like a goldfish or hamster.

The joys of pet ownership come with certain responsibilities. Bringing a pet into your home and your neighborhood obligates you to care for and train the pet properly. For example, a dog must be housebroken, taught to obey your commands, and trained to behave appropriately when he encounters other people or animals. Owners must also be mindful of their pet's particular nutritional and medical needs.

The purpose of the OUR BEST FRIENDS series is to provide a helpful and comprehensive introduction to pet ownership. Each book contains the basic information a prospective pet owner needs in order to choose the right pet for his or her situation and to care for that pet throughout the pet's lifetime. Training, socialization, proper nutrition, potential medical issues, and the legal responsibilities of pet ownership are thoroughly explained and discussed, and an abundance of expert tips and suggestions are offered. Whether it is a hamster, corn snake, guinea pig, or Labrador Retriever, the books in the OUR BEST FRIENDS series provide everything the reader needs to know about how to have a happy, well-adjusted, and well-behaved pet.

CHAPTER ONE

Is a Cat Right for You?

Versatile, adaptable, and delightfully affectionate, the domestic cat is one of the most beloved pets in the world. It is the most common pet in the United States, surpassing even the dog in popularity. Most cats in the world are mixed breed cats. Just a small minority, as little as 1 percent of the cat population, is recognized as pedigreed.

Mixed breed cats offer an infinite variety of characteristics, colors, and personalities. Some are longhaired and others are shorthaired. Some have patterned fur coats and others are solid. No two are exactly the same. There is a one-of-a-kind feline to meet every person's ideal.

Although each domestic cat is endowed with its own individual physical and personality traits, there are some characteristics from the genus *Felis catus* that all cats share. It is these similarities—not their differences—that make all cats such popular pets.

WHY CATS MAKE GREAT PETS

What is it that gives the cat so much appeal? In a nutshell, cats possess ideal qualities that allow them to live harmoniously with humans. Of all the furry, cuddly, affectionate pet choices available, cats are among the most interactive, easy to care for, and practical for most living situations.

Cats make great pets for city dwellers because of their small size and independent nature. Unlike some other pets, cats won't mind being left home alone during the day.

Cats can live in apartments in the city. They can live in homes in the suburbs. They are comfortable on farms, fulfilling their duties as vermin eradicators. As indoor pets cats can live just about anywhere their humans choose to live. And with their quiet, nondestructive, and unassuming presence, cats are much more acceptable to neighbors than some other kinds of pets. This is especially true in areas where humans live in close proximity to each other.

While mixed breed cats come in a great variety, they all fall within a sensible size range. Cats, in general, are neither too large nor too small. They are large enough to hug and small enough to carry. They don't eat much, they don't take up much room on the bed or couch, and they make exceptional lap warmers. Cats don't need to be handled as carefully as hamsters or gerbils. And they won't knock people over if they jump on them, as a large dog would.

Best of all, cats can be reliably litter box trained. You don't have to keep your pet confined to a cage as you would with a rabbit or guinea pig. And you don't have to worry about letting the cat out several times a day as you would with a dog. A litter box–trained cat is a low maintenance pet that can fit into a busy lifestyle with a minimum of inconvenience.

The independent nature of the cat is one of her greatest assets. Less demanding and more self-sufficient than a dog, a cat isn't as prone to separation anxiety or other behavior problems when left home alone during the work day. Cats love human attention, but they do not require copious amounts of it. The feline is an undeniably great match for people with busy lifestyles.

PHYSICAL NEEDS

As seamlessly as cats tend to fit into the human world, they can only do so when their needs are met. They need food, water, shelter, exercise, and health care. Even their self-groomed coat requires some attention. It takes time and money to meet all these needs. When it comes to kitty keeping, are you willing to put enough into it in order to get the maximum benefits out of it?

FOOD: If you want to keep your kitty purring for many years, you need to feed your feline friend a nutritious diet. Contrary to an old myth, cats cannot live on a saucer of milk alone. In fact, milk can upset an adult cat's digestion system. You need to feed your cat appropriate cat food.

Most animals thrive when they are fed at regular times each day. Fortunately, cats tend to be a little more forgiving than other pets if dinner comes late once in a while. This is an advantage for owners with demanding careers. Even so, if your job duties interfere with your cat's eating schedule, you may want to look into buying an automatic cat feeder.

Fresh water is extremely important for your furry friend. Although cats do not need a lot of water, they do require fresh water on a daily basis. Even if it doesn't look like your cat has drunk any water from her bowl, you need to refill it. When water sits out in the open, it can start to taste foul because of bacteria, and your cat may refuse to drink it. Cats can suffer serious urinary problems if they stop drinking water.

SHELTER: What kind of shelter can you offer a cat? Cats may be exceptionally adaptable to outdoor living, but pet cats are safest when kept indoors. Cats that are allowed to roam outdoors face many risks of injury or death. They are vulnerable to being attacked by other animals, getting hit by a car, or ingesting poisons. Unless you live on a farm, you probably don't need a "working" cat to keep the rodent population under control. You can, however, provide outdoor experiences for your cat by constructing a safe outdoor enclosure or by training your cat to accept a leash.

EXERCISE: Even if your cat is kept indoors, she can get enough exercise to stay healthy. Cats sleep approximately 16 hours per day and have very modest exercise requirements. Keeping your cat active shouldn't require much of your time. And there are many simple ways to keep your indoor cat physically active. A paper grocery bag, a cardboard box, or a Ping-Pong ball can become a plaything that will delight your cat. Although cats love to share playtime with their owners, they're also good at exercising by themselves.

HEALTH CARE: Health care is the most expensive part of having a pet cat. This is especially true during the first year, when a series of vaccinations and surgical sterilization of the

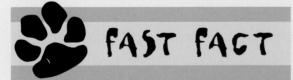

FAST FACT

Giving less food to a cat will not increase her drive to hunt. The hunting instinct is so strong in the cat that it will hunt even when well fed.

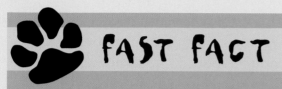

FAST FACT

The domestic cat has over 60,000 hairs per square inch on its body. No wonder cats are so soft to the touch!

male (neutering) or female (spaying) is necessary. It's a good idea to plan for these expenses by contacting veterinary clinics in your area before you bring your pet home.

GROOMING: One of the best ways you can help your veterinarian keep your kitty healthy is to regularly groom your pet. The amount of time and effort needed for this task depends on the hair characteristics of your mixed breed cat. Longhair cats will require daily brushing. Shorthaired cats can be brushed once a week.

But grooming isn't just about hair. You also need to trim your cat's claws and provide dental care. Does this sound like too much work? Just remember that the strength of a human-animal bond relates directly to the amount of time spent caring for the animal.

EMOTIONAL NEEDS

Obviously, it's essential to meet your cat's physical needs. But did

you know that cats have emotional needs, too? Cats are living, breathing, and thinking creatures. For optimal mental health they require the following:

COMPANIONSHIP: Cats do not demand as much human interaction as dogs. But to be socialized they still need significant contact with people. Cats that are emotionally neglected

Developing a strong bond with your cat begins with making her feel safe and secure. Gentle and loving physical contact will create a good foundation for building trust.

may grow to distrust people. Some may become feral, or wild. When you get a cat for companionship, don't forget that the companionship needs to go both ways.

SAFETY AND SECURITY: Mixed breed cats come in all types of personalities, and their individual emotional needs will vary. Bold and outgoing cats will feel perfectly secure in their own right. More reserved and sensitive cats may require you to make an effort to ensure they feel safe and secure. One way to do this is to provide a high perch, where the cat can observe the surroundings from a safe height. Also, cats do not particularly enjoy having to share living space with other animals that threaten them. Be sure to consider whether your existing pets will tolerate having a cat living with them.

TERRITORY: By instinct, cats are naturally territorial creatures. They will often choose certain areas to be their favorite "hangouts." This is especially true if there are other cats or pets in the household. Be sure you have enough room in your home so that all the four-legged members of the family can have their own space.

ENVIRONMENTAL ENRICHMENT: Being mentally healthy also means being mentally active. Animals get bored when there's nothing to do. Worse than that, they can get lazy and fat. It's important to keep house cats active and stimulated by providing environmental enrichment. Keep your kitty entertained by getting her a new toy once in awhile. Other ways to enrich your cat's environment include putting cat perches by your windows, spending time playing with your cat, and making her hunt for treats.

CHILDREN AND CATS

Cats make wonderful companions for children. And having a pet cat can provide you with numerous opportunities for teaching kids how to handle animals properly. These skills will benefit children their entire lives.

Older children especially tend to get along well with cats. Because cat care is not as demanding as dog care, kids can take responsibility for caring for the new pet without much trouble. Still, it is always a good idea

FAST FACT

Cats are crepuscular animals. This means they are most active during twilight, the hours between daylight and darkness.

An adult must always supervise young children with kittens and cats. This will help keep both the child and the pet from accidentally getting hurt.

for parents to provide support and guidance to make sure the cat is provided for properly. When an animal moves into your household, it should be considered the family pet, not just a child's pet.

With younger children, it is important to prevent injuries to both kids and kitties. Young children should never be left unattended with any pet. A child under the age of five

or six may not realize that cats feel pain. A toddler may not have the motor skills to handle a cat gently. Either the cat or the child could end up becoming injured. But this doesn't mean young children must be denied the wonderful experience of kitty companionship. They can still have opportunities to play with cats, pet them, and help care for them. It is just that they'll need supervision

and guidance from a parent when doing so.

OTHER PETS AND CATS

Whether or not your mixed breed cat will get along with other pets depends entirely on the cat. When raised with rats, mice, or hamsters, some cats have defied their natural instinct to kill prey. Instead they become very good friends with these animals. This is why, if you already have other pets, it is often a good idea to get a kitten instead of a full-grown cat. If your other pets don't frighten the kitten, she may grow up to develop unique relationships with all different kinds of animals.

Adult cats can be a different story. Some adult cats are very particular about their animal friends. Others are more open-minded. A very sensitive cat might find the clamorous antics of a dog intolerable. However, a rough-and-tumble feline might be very receptive to the idea of having a rowdy canine playmate.

Even when it comes to socializing with members of their own species, cats can be choosy. But when they are introduced to each other slowly and carefully, they can often be convinced to get along. So plan on having a trial period to be sure pets and people alike can adjust to having a new feline family member. Household harmony is important for the health and happiness of everyone in your home. If conflicts are making everyone miserable, you may have to find a more suitable home for your new pet.

PET OWNER RESPONSIBILITIES

It is important to take proper care of your cat and ensure that she fits comfortably into your home and

Dogs and cats can live together but they'll need to be supervised at first so that they don't "play" too rough.

lifestyle. But owning a cat isn't just about you and your pet. There is a much larger responsibility—the overpopulation of cats in the world. To avoid contributing to this problem responsible cat owners do not allow their cats to have litters. And they make sure to have their male cats neutered and female cats spayed.

Also keep in mind that cats live an average of 18 to 22 years. Deciding to share your life with a cat is a lengthy commitment. That decision should not be made impulsively. It is neither responsible nor in the best interest of the animal to acquire a cat if you cannot provide a stable, long-term home. Be sure you are prepared to make this commitment.

You also need to consider the impact your new cat can have on the people who live outside your home. For instance, if you live in an apartment, your cat's midnight serenades might disturb your neighbors. If you live in a house and let your pet outdoors, you can upset neighbors if the cat hunts at their bird feeder or uses their garden as a toilet. Be prepared to seek help for behavior issues that inconvenience or intrude on the lives of others. If you decide to let your cat outside, it is best to keep your pet confined to your own property, preferably in a safe enclosure.

Remember to be considerate when you have guests in your home, too. Some people don't like cats. There are also those who are severely allergic.

Your outdoor cat may love to "sing" for the neighbors at all hours. It's your job as a responsible pet owner to make sure that the sound of your pet yowling does not disturb others.

APPROXIMATE FIRST-YEAR COSTS TO MAINTAIN A CAT

Collar and ID tag	$15	Vet office and exam charges	$130
Litter and litter box	$175	Neutering or spaying	$200
Food	$125	TOTAL	$885
Toys	$20		
Bed	$20		
Pet carrier	$25		
Grooming supplies	$25		
Kitten vaccinations (series)	$150		

(These costs are a conservative estimate and do not include adoption fees. Always investigate the costs and be prepared for the financial responsibilities of owning a pet.)

So don't force your guests to tolerate unwanted attention from your social feline. Keep her in a separate room.

Abiding by pet owner etiquette benefits everybody, including your pet. Aside from maintaining good neighborly relations, you will be allowing people to develop a true appreciation of your favorite feline.

When your pet leaves only good impressions, everybody is happy.

❧❧❧

The mixed breed cat is versatile, adaptable, and delightfully affectionate. As you learn more about this extraordinary animal, you'll discover why the cat is one of the most beloved pets in the world!

CHAPTER TWO

History of Cats

The cat has been praised over the centuries for her beauty and elegance, her stealth and athleticism, and her intelligence and affection. How and why did the cat become such a refined and beguiling creature? How did the cat develop from being a wild creature to a domesticated one? Most perplexing, how did humans develop a friendship with an animal that appears to prefer independence to alliance? Over time, numerous breeds of cat exhibiting a variety of characteristics have been developed. But the cat has retained her aura of mystery and grace, and

Domesticated cats have a long history that leads back to ancient Egypt. In that ancient civilization, cats were revered as having godlike qualities and were favorite pets of the pharaohs.

her lithe form and invariable instincts have remained intact.

WHAT IS A CAT?

The abilities of the cat have long captured the imagination of novelists and poets. Cats have been the subjects of myths and legends, and even superstitions. The domestic cat exhibits a unique combination of characteristics and unusual abilities that continue to mystify many people today.

PHYSICAL ABILITIES: Cats don't need infrared goggles to see in the dark. Their mesmerizing slit eyes were not made for beauty. They allow the cat to see in near total darkness—and stalk prey at night.

The cat's eye has a 20 percent higher ratio of rods (light receptors) to cones (color receptors) than a human eye. This makes it easy for cats to prowl in dim light. The physiology of the cat's eye also means that the animal is not attracted to brightly colored objects, such as toys. Color doesn't mean much to a predator that hunts camouflaged prey.

The cat's ability to see in extremely low-light conditions is remarkable. But even in pitch-blackness, the cat still manages to get around. She has another unique tool for pussyfooting through the dark. The cat's long whiskers serve as hypersensitive feelers. Twelve whiskers on each side of the muzzle and several above each eye

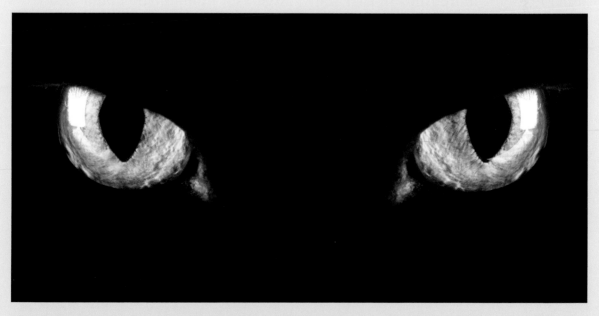

The iconic image of a cat's eyes. Cats are actually able to see in near-darkness, so that they can maneuver and stalk prey at night.

FAST FACT

Cats don't see well up close. Sometimes they develop the habit of bumping their water dishes or swatting the water to create waves. This makes it is easier for them to sense the surface of the water with their whiskers, and they avoid dunking their noses when they take a drink.

effectively tell the cat where she can or cannot go.

The cat even has a couple of feelers on the back of each foreleg. These help her test her footing or feel her prey. Despite having extraordinary vision capabilities, the cat has some eyesight limitations in that she is somewhat farsighted. That is, close objects are not in focus. The cat's eyes can easily locate prey at a distance, but it is difficult for her to see something right under her nose.

A feline also has enhanced senses of hearing and smell. Cats can hear high-pitched sounds up to 100,000 cycles per second, while humans are capable of hearing only 20,000. The cat's sense of smell is also strong, but not because it is necessary for hunting. Scents are important to cats in a social context. They use scent glands to mark territories and search for mates.

Cats have scent glands on the side of their faces, at the base of their tails, and on the bottoms of their feet. If you ever wondered why your cat likes to rub her face against you when she's happy to see you, it's because she's marking you with a "friendly" scent. The same can be said when she rubs against your leg with her wrap-around tail. When a cat scratches on her scratching post, she's not just conditioning her claws. She is marking the post with an "I was here" scent.

As phenomenal as a cat's senses are, her most incredible abilities may actually lie in her physical prowess. The cat is the Superman of domestic animals. If she were as large as a human, she could easily leap over a building in a single bound. After all, cats can jump heights that are five times their body length. This ability is a valuable talent for a creature that seeks out high places to reach safety and for surveying her territory.

FAST FACT

When a cat rubs or butts its head on you, she is exhibiting bunting behavior. She is "marking" you with a friendly scent from the scent glands on her head.

Cats have an incredible sense of balance and can easily traverse even the narrowest of walkways, such as this handrail.

With this fondness for high places, cats necessarily have to possess significant abilities of balance and coordination. Cats can walk effortlessly atop fences and tree branches. If they should fall from a great height, they have a unique "righting reflex" that allows them to land safely on their feet. Such abilities are possible because of the animal's unique construction. Cats have extremely flexible spines. They possess five more vertebrae—the small bones of the backbone—than humans. They also have no collar-bone to inhibit the movement of their shoulders. This allows a cat to be as flaccid as a wet towel.

The forepaws are another feature that helps the cat stay comfortable in high places. A cat's claws are retractable, so they are always sharp

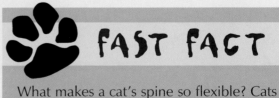

FAST FACT

What makes a cat's spine so flexible? Cats have five more vertebrae than humans!

and ready. Unlike the nails of a dog, a cat's claws do not wear down when walked on. The cat can easily hang from anything its claws hook into because there is so much strength in those dexterous, prey-snaring forepaws.

Perhaps the only drawback to such a perfect tool is that, while cat claws are great for climbing up trees, they are not designed very well for coming back down. Unlike squirrels, cats cannot fold their hind legs backward to climb down a tree headfirst.

Most cats learn to descend backwards, and to jump from branch to branch, in order to get down. Young cats that are new to the art of tree climbing, however, sometimes get stuck and require human assistance.

FELINE PSYCHOLOGY: As remarkable as they are, the cat's physical features exist for one reason and one reason only—survival. Similarly, the animal's psychological traits are deeply rooted in the purpose of survival. As the cat evolved over the centuries, those

As your kitten grows, she may find herself stuck in a tree or two. If this happens, don't panic. Though you may have to manually remove her the first time, she will eventually learn the proper way to come down without human help.

characteristics unnecessary for survival either remained undeveloped or faded away.

The primitive cat did not need to hunt in packs, like dogs, in order to survive. That is why today's cat is more of a solitary, independent creature. Cats are quite capable of forming bonds with other creatures, but they do so on their own terms. Unlike dogs, which *need* to bond with humans, cats *choose* to make friends with people.

Another result of the evolutionary survival of the cat is its strong territorial instinct. The purpose of establishing a territory and defending it against interlopers is related to the cat's need to protect its food source. Too many predators in the same territory can result in a life-threatening shortage of food.

A by-product of this territorial instinct is the cat's preference for a stable, familiar environment. Cats tend to be enormously stressed by changes in their territory, such as home remodeling, rearrangement of furniture, or a move to a new home. The stress can cause the cat to have litter box lapses, become aggressive, or exhibit other changes in behavior.

To assert control over her territory the cat typically possesses some level of dominance. Dominance is used to defend personal space, but it

FELINE BODY LANGUAGE

Relaxed: Ears forward and slightly dropped to the side, tail level to the body or lower, posture neither elevated nor crouched.

Happy: Ears forward, eyes slightly squinted; walks with tail held straight up with the tip bent.

Irritated: Ears flat out to the sides, crouched body, tail flicking from side to side.

Angry: Ears back flat, arched back, hair on back raised, and whiskers bristled.

Frightened: Ears flattened back, pupils dilated, body crouched, spitting or hissing.

Aroused (hunting instinct triggered): Facial expression keenly alert; pricked ears, wide eyes, semi-crouched body, and tail twitching low.

is also used in the process of acquiring mates. A cat's sex life involves fighting, caterwauling (howling), and scent marking (spraying urine on objects). If you don't want your cat exhibiting these undesirable behaviors, you should have your pet neutered or spayed.

PREHISTORIC CATS

Scientists believe that the amazing physical abilities and psychological traits of cats are the result of centuries of evolution. It is theorized that both cats and dogs came from the same ancestors—small, tree-dwelling carnivores called miacids. These creatures existed about 60 million years ago. They were about the same size as modern housecats, but they had longer bodies and shorter legs. Their prick ears and tree-climbing ability served them well, ensuring their continued survival.

According to paleontologists from the Smithsonian Institute, about 48 million years ago the miacids evolved into two separate lines. From the

A model of *Megantereon cultridens*, a prehistoric cat that existed 30 million years ago. Aside from the long canine teeth, a slightly longer neck, and a shorter lumbar region of the spine, this ancient feline is similar in appearance to that of modern cats.

Miacidae came dogs and bears. And from the Viverravidae came cats, hyenas, and several other predators. The first cat-type animal to evolve from Viverravidae was Proailurus, which appeared about 30 million years ago. This animal still possessed the long-bodied, short-legged form of miacids. From Proailurus came Pseudailurus, and from Pseudalilurus came Schizailurus. Then, about 18 million years ago, Schizailurus gave rise to the Felidae family, from which domestic cats are descended. The first of the small cats, Felis, came on the scene around 12 million years ago.

Even though domestic cats are far removed from their larger cousins (by millions of years), they still appear to have much in common with them. Petting a cat is, in some ways, like touching a lion. Observing a cat on the hunt is akin to watching cheetahs in Africa attack prey or jaguars in South America on the prowl. As you will discover, you can take the cat out of the wild, but you cannot take the wild out of the cat!

CATS OF EGYPT

The first domestic cat, *Felis catus*, appeared in Egypt about 5,000 years ago. It is not known which species of wildcat evolved to become the domestic cat we know today. It's possible that several species were

FAST FACT

While large cats, like lions and tigers, can purr by exhaling air, domestic cats can purr while exhaling and inhaling.

interbred at some time to create a unique hybrid. However, most experts believe the African wildcat, *Felis lybica*, which was plentiful in North Africa and easy to tame, was the forebear of shorthaired domestic cats. Other animals that may have contributed to the domestic cat's gene pool at some time are the Asian wildcat, *Felis manul*, and the European wildcat, *Felis silvestris*.

It is impossible to know how and when the first cat and human formed a bond. What is known is that ancient Egyptians had become experts in agricultural production at the time. They were producing and storing great stockpiles of grain, which most likely attracted vermin like rats and mice. Vermin, in turn, were attractive to predators like cats. Witnessing the deft efficiency with which cats exterminated granary pests, Egyptians probably offered incentives to encourage cats to hang around. They may have put food out to attract cats or attempted to tame the litters of kittens they found.

In the ancient world, people often honored their cats through art such as carvings, paintings, and pottery. This decorative 10th century terracotta dish depicts a hare and a feline-type animal.

Eventually, the attempts at domestication were successful.

Cats quickly became highly valued in Egyptian culture. People were enthralled with the cat's mystical powers—her ability to see in the dark, incredible stealth, and noble attitude. Soon the cat was raised in status to that of a god, associated with Bastet, the Egyptian lioness war goddess. In fact, the cat was believed to have such close ties to divinity that priests would analyze the movements and behaviors of cats in order to make predictions about the future.

Cats in Egypt were so treasured that they were given much respect when they died. Their remains were often mummified, and they were buried with food and toys for the afterlife. A family that lost a cat went into a period of mourning, and grieving members even shaved their eyebrows. So revered were Egyptian cats that it was illegal to export them. But all the powers of Pharaoh could not keep such a good thing isolated from the rest of the world.

LANDING IN EUROPE

Phoenician sailors are credited with assisting the cat's exodus from Egypt. Some of these seagoers may have taken cats aboard their ships to protect their goods from vermin. But it's almost certain the sailors also discovered a lucrative trade in smuggling cats. The elegant and unusual creatures could fetch a substantial sum in other lands. But it is also likely that the cat's propensity to stow away in small spaces may have led to her travels aboard a Phoenician ship.

It was the cat's destiny to find her way throughout the human world, one way or another. As the Romans conquered lands around the Mediterranean Sea from 300–100 B.C., they also helped to populate the European continent with cats. But although the cat was initially well received in foreign lands, her heyday of royal treatment soon came to an end.

During the early Middle Ages (circa A.D. 1100 to 1450), the once-revered domestic cat fell out of favor

FAST FACT

Psi-trailing is the name given to the phenomenon where cats find their owners over long distances through unfamiliar territory. This is a type of extrasensory perception that is not fully understood.

in Europe. These were difficult times for humans and cats alike. Many civilizations were in upheaval due to wars. As superstitious humans looked for a cause of their misery, cats became associated with the devil and witchcraft. They were shunned, tortured, and killed.

During the 1300s, the Black Death gripped Europe with a devastating and deadly plague. This flea-borne disease is spread by rats, a

Cats found popularity at sea and during the middle ages because of their ability to hunt and kill disease carrying rats and mice.

favorite prey of cats. But at the same time, Europeans were killing cats because of fears and superstitions, allowing the rats to thrive. The plague ultimately decimated a third of the human population in Europe.

Cats in Europe continued to be persecuted for another 300 years. But they were not driven to extinction. In other parts of the world, including the Middle East and Asia, cats were still prized for their hunting ability and appreciated for their affinity to humans.

By the 1700s, cats had found their way back into the good graces of the Europeans. People admired the many different colors, patterns, and forms of domestic cats. The mid- to late-1800s saw the development of groups that exhibited domesticated animals. People began to organize horse shows, dog shows, small animal shows, and even cat shows.

Cat clubs began to spring up in response to the need for a registration system for pedigreed and purebred cats. In order to create a standardized central organization for the appreciation, promotion, and breeding of cats, the Governing Council of the Cat Fancy (GCCF) was formed in 1910 in the United Kingdom. Cat enthusiasts finally had a framework for identifying, producing and exhibiting purebred cats. The GCCF currently consists of 146 affiliated cat clubs.

CATS IN THE UNITED STATES

Cats probably arrived in North America as early as the 1500s. They most likely accompanied Spanish, English, and French explorers aboard sailing vessels, where they were kept for hunting rodents. The cats also served as mousers for the colonists who took up farming in the Americas. Although their undeserved bad reputation in Europe as consorts of witches followed them at first, they soon enjoyed more positive attention.

By the late 1800s, Americans were following European trends. People in the United States embraced the idea of cat shows, and in 1895 the nation's first cat show was held at Madison Square Garden in New York City. At that time, there were no distinguishable breeds. Cats were categorized according to "type," such as Longhair, Domestic Shorthair, and Foreign Shorthair. There weren't any cat clubs or registries, so there were very few rules as to which animals could or could not be shown. Any type of cat could be entered, and both neutered and intact animals were allowed.

The first cat club in the United States, the Beresford Cat Club, was formed in Chicago in 1899. This club, which was renamed the American Cat Association in 1901, took on the responsibility of registering cat breeds. Disagreements among the ranks led one faction of this group to form its own organization, the Cat Fanciers' Association (CFA), in 1906.

Since then, several other cat registries have also been established. The American Cat Fanciers' Association (ACFA) was founded in 1955, and the International Cat Association (TICA) was formed in 1979. Several regional registries have also been established since then. Depending on their needs and goals, cat fanciers may register their cats with one or more of these organizations. This means there are plenty of venues from which to choose for those interested in showing their cats.

You don't need to own a pedigreed cat to participate in a cat show. Your mixed breed cat can be entered in Household Pet classes. This category was established in appreciation of the many fine feline specimens without pedigrees. Household Pet entrants are judged on their uniqueness, condition, and appearance. But they are held to an especially high standard when it comes to temperament. If you think your mixed breed cat has the right physical traits and personality to dazzle the judges,

Judge Diana Doernberg holds a cat at the annual Cat Championship, sponsored by the Cat Fanciers' Association. There are many different types of cat shows and you don't necessarily need a pedigreed cat to enter.

check with the various registries to find out what their individual requirements are for this class.

MODERN CATS

Participating in cat shows has become an engaging hobby for

Because cats prefer to fend for themselves and don't require much care, they make great pets for older people.

many cat lovers, but cats play many more roles in people's lives today. Cats will probably never give up their job of hunting rodents, whether they live on a farm or in a city. This is a profession for which they have incredible passion, to the point of being obsessed. Even well-fed cats will hunt for the sheer sport of it. But although they are useful and talented in this field, cats are appreciated even more for their comfortable companionship.

The companionship of cats brings comfort to the elderly and infirm in nursing homes. Cats are a calming presence in libraries, veterinary clinics, and other places of business. They provide a link to normalcy for those who are institutionalized. And cats bring happiness, stress relief, and health benefits into our own homes.

ﻬﻬﻬ

Entertaining, affectionate and easy to care for, the domestic cat is sure to possess a secure hold on human hearts in the years to come.

CHAPTER THREE

The Best Possible Beginning

When you start out with quality ingredients, the soup always turns out better. When it comes to life with your cat, good beginnings tend to result in good endings too. Do you know where to find the kitty with the right seasoning for your lifestyle? How do you

taste test your choices to know you're getting just the right cat for you? And how do you choose a veterinarian who can help you preserve the wonderful flavor you and your pet make together?

The choices you make in the beginning can affect the entire future

Choosing a kitten can be tough, especially when they're all so cute!

of your feline friendship. So be sure to consider all your options ahead of time and let good judgment and common sense guide you. Don't be surprised if your heart interjects a few feelings, too. Sometimes you just "know" when a match is right.

WHERE TO FIND A CAT

Because cats are amazingly prolific, the supply of mixed breed cats is abundant. There are many places to find them—animal shelters, rescues, breeders, pet shops, farms, and even the Internet. But while location, convenience, and cost are all important considerations, the most important thing is finding a source that offers healthy, socialized cats.

ANIMAL SHELTERS: If you have a hard time choosing among all the different varieties of products at the supermarket, you will probably be completely

Animal shelters, rescue organizations, and other sources of mixed breed cats can be located through the Internet. However, never purchase a cat online without first seeing the cat in person. It is impossible to judge the health and condition of an animal until you see it for yourself.

Not sure where to find cat adoption agencies in your area? Check the petfinder.com Web site. This site can also help you locate the specific kind of mixed breed cat you're looking for.

overwhelmed at the animal shelter. There, you'll typically find a good supply of cats looking for new homes, and it may be difficult to choose from among all the wonderful feline specimens. On the plus side, you have a very good chance of finding that one special feline friend (or two!).

In addition to the large selection of potential pets, there are many other benefits. Adopting a cat from an animal shelter is cost-effective, since adoption fees are exceptionally reasonable. Most shelter adult cats are up to date on vaccinations and have already been neutered or spayed. Kittens that have not been neutered or spayed often come with vouchers that help you offset the significant expense of these procedures. There are always start-up costs involved in kitty keeping, but the adoption choice offers the best value.

Many shelters temperament-test their animals to make sure they are placed in the right homes. This can

Adoption is a great option if you're looking for a new feline friend. There are literally hundreds of cats and kittens that need homes every day. If you're looking for a cat, try stopping by your local shelter, pound, or rescue organization.

be useful if you have any children or other pets in your household. Do you need a cat that is not fearful of dogs? Do you need a cat that is tolerant of children and not overly sensitive to the noise of child play? Do you need a cat that is good with other cats? The shelter staff can help you find the best kitty to meet your needs.

If you find your ideal cat at a shelter, you'll be required to sign an adoption contract that specifies the kind of care and living conditions you must provide for your adopted

FAST FACT

Kittens are typically in higher demand than adult cats. But don't overlook the many benefits of adopting an adult cat. Kittens are babies, and as such they demand much more time and attention than a grown cat does. They must be more highly supervised and they must be trained. Do you have the time to devote to raising a baby cat? Or would you be happier with an older, calmer kitty that can fit into your home and lifestyle with a minimum of effort?

pet. These contracts are tools of the animal welfare trade that help ensure adopted animals are treated with kindness and respect. You should read the adoption contract thoroughly to be sure its requirements are agreeable to you. Every organization drafts its own adoption contract, and provisions may differ from one animal shelter to another.

RESCUE ORGANIZATIONS: Rescue organizations basically provide the same services as animal shelters. They help place homeless animals in permanent homes. However, rather than operate from a central kennel facility, rescues often consist of a network of foster homes. This type of arrangement is especially beneficial to cats, which are prone to stress in a typical shelter environment. When a cat is in a comfortable home situation, foster workers can evaluate the animal's personality more easily.

While a foster arrangement is better for a cat, it is not always ideal for cat adopters. Because cats are kept at different locations, you will need to travel in order to meet potential pets. Then again, foster families are able to develop more personal relationships with the cats in their care. They are able to provide more detailed insights into each cat's likes, dislikes, and habits.

Most rescue organizations are run by dedicated and knowledgeable volunteers. But keep in mind that respectable nonprofit organizations cannot be run on good intentions alone. Anyone who loves cats can start his or her own cat rescue, even if lacking the experience or financial resources to provide proper care for the animals. If a rescue group doesn't appear to be professionally managed, find another source for your pet.

BREEDERS: Breeders do not raise only pedigreed cats. Just as there are dog breeders who produce mixed breed dogs to meet public demand, there are cat breeders who raise mixed breed cats with specific characteristics. Some breeders may specialize in so-called oriental-type cats, some may produce longhaired varieties, and some may produce domestic cats with popular colors or markings.

There are some advantages in getting a cat from a breeder. You can find the type of cat with the physical and temperamental characteristics you really want. You won't have to guess what your kitten will look like as an adult. And you can evaluate the parent cats and the environment in which the kittens were raised.

Unfortunately, there is one monumental problem with purchasing a cat from this source. Every time someone buys a mixed breed cat from a breeder, that sale creates a demand for continued breeding in a world that is already grossly overpopulated with mixed breed cats. Chances are, there is already a cat with the characteristics you desire awaiting adoption in a shelter somewhere. If your conscience doesn't discourage you from purchasing from a breeder, perhaps the higher price of purchasing a cat from this source will.

OTHER SOURCES: Pet shops will occasionally have a supply of mixed breed cats for sale. These are usually the product of accidental or irresponsible breeding. Pet owners who do not get their female cats spayed eventually end up with a basketful of kittens. They become window dressing for the nearest pet shop. Although you might be able to find nice pet quality kittens in a local pet store, you should carefully evaluate the kittens for health and temperament. And make sure the pet shop offers a health guarantee.

Some of the larger pet store outlets have embraced an adoption-friendly alternative to selling kittens. They host various adoption events or provide space during weekends for rescue organizations to show their adoptable animals. Adopters can

find great pets and get all the supplies they need for kitty keeping in one stop. People find wonderful feline companions, homeless cats find homes, and the pet store enjoys greater sales. It's a win-win-win situation!

While driving through the country, you might have seen a sign out by the road offering cats for free. You find the farm kittens sitting picturesquely on a bale of hay next to the barn, begging passersby to take them home. Although the price is hard to resist, you need to remember that nothing is really free.

Kittens that are kept outdoors are sure to be riddled with parasites, most likely fleas and intestinal

Farm kittens may be cute, but they are more likely to have health problems, which will cost more money in the long run.

worms. They also could be carrying serious diseases like feline distemper or feline leukemia (FeLV). Farm cats typically don't receive good quality diets or veterinary care, which has a huge impact on their physical health. Even more important, outdoor cats and their kittens do not always get the human attention that indoor cats do. Farm cats may not be as well socialized to people.

Not all farm kittens are unsociable health disasters, though. Every situation is unique. Still, you should be cautious about getting a free kitten from any source. Listen to your head and not your heart on this one. And be prepared to face the risks of taking on a kitten with a questionable health history.

CHOOSING A CAT

The task of choosing a cat isn't as difficult as it seems. Just be sure to put a little bit of thought into it ahead of time. Think about the age, gender, number, and individual characteristics of the perfect cat for you. You may be open-minded about some of these qualifications. But there is one thing you should not be willing to compromise on—health. No matter what type of cat you choose, you should make sure a prospective pet is healthy before you bring it home.

KITTEN OR ADULT: There are a number of good reasons to start off with a kitten. If you have other pets, a kitten may be accepted more readily by the existing four-legged members of the family. While kittens can be wild and annoying at times, they tend to stimulate the nurturing instincts in other animals—even dogs! And kittens, likewise, learn to get along better with other pets when raised with them.

However, a kitten is a good choice only if you can put the time and effort into rearing her. You'll have to teach her to use a scratching post, how to play without biting or scratching, and

Be sure you are ready for the commitment a cute kitten requires before bringing one home.

other household rules. You'll have to be extra vigilant in supervising your tiny tiger to keep her safe, because if "curiosity killed the cat," it can literally consume a kitten. And don't forget the health care costs for a kitten are significantly higher than those for an adult cat.

If a kitten is your choice, the best time to scout around for a new companion is in late spring and early summer. Shelter personnel refer to this period as "kitten season" because so many kittens are born during this time of year. If you look for your new pet during kitten season, you'll have many choices from which to choose. You may also find that many shelters offer reduced adoption fees for kittens or other adoption incentives to help relieve shelter overcrowding.

If your situation isn't necessarily dependent on getting a kitten, don't be afraid to consider the many benefits of adopting an adult cat. There are many, many adoptable mixed

FAST FACT

Whether you intend to or not, you have hired a vermin exterminator when you bring a cat into your home! Cats never lose their drive to hunt, and in the absence of mice or other rodents, your cat may think it's her duty to dispatch any bugs she finds crawling about the house.

breed cats that would make excellent pets. Adult cats are generally calmer and quieter than kittens. But the best part of choosing a "ready-made" cat is that it takes far less effort to assimilate your new pet into your life.

MALE OR FEMALE: With cats, there are some differences between the sexes when it comes to size and behavior. This doesn't mean that one gender is better than the other. It just means there are differences between male and female cats. Each should be appreciated for its own special qualities.

Male cats, also called "toms," tend to be a little larger than females. Toms generally like to play rough. They can be particularly rowdy during adolescence—between 6 months and 2 years of age. Toms also tend to be more outgoing than females, especially with people. If

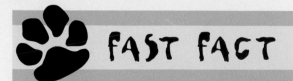

FAST FACT

Approximately 15 percent of kittens resist socialization to humans. These felines never learn to appreciate human handling, but they may express affection in ways other than physical contact.

you like the attention of an exceptionally friendly feline, you might want to consider a male cat. Just be prepared to give him an equal amount of attention in return.

Females, also called "queens," tend to be much more sensitive and independent. If you want a cat that is gentler and less demanding, a female might be a better choice. Keep in mind that these are generalizations of gender differences. There are many nongender-related personality traits that can influence a cat's behavior. Cats are extremely individualistic. It's very possible to find a female that is both gentle and outgoing, or a male that is both rough-and-tumble and nondemanding.

ONE OR TWO: According to a 2007 study by the American Veterinary Medical Association, cats outnumber dogs in the United States. The organization reports that there are 81 million cats, as compared to 72 million dogs. Yet, cats occupy fewer homes than dogs. That's because the average number of cats per household is more than two, while the average number of dogs per household is less than two. Obviously, many people have discovered the

If you decide to adopt two cats, some experts feel it's best to choose a male and female. With two cats of the same gender, there is a greater chance that they'll fight over territory. To eliminate the chance of unwanted kittens, have them spayed or neutered.

distinct advantages of having more than one cat.

Cats make great companions for humans, but they also make great companions for each other. Kittens, in particular, appreciate having a playmate that will play with them on their own level. A kitten without a feline buddy can get into a consider-able amount of mischief. It is better to have your kitty expend her energy wrestling with a playmate than climbing your living room drapes! Kittens raised together will become bonded friends for life.

There are also many adult "bond-ed pairs" available for adoption. These cats have already established a close relationship, so you don't have to worry about how they will react to each other. Best of all, many shelters offer discounted adoption fees when you adopt a bonded pair.

If you are interested in adopting two cats that are unfamiliar to each other, you will have to evaluate each cat's personality carefully to deter-mine if the two will be a good match. Adult cats can be very choosy about their friends. Sometimes it's best to have a trial introduction period to see if the two animals will get along with each other.

Getting two cats means double the purrs, double the fun, and double the joy in your life. But it also means

FAST FACT

If you have other pets, it's best to bring home a new cat on a trial basis to make sure all the animals will get along with each other.

double the expense. For the most part, cats are economical pets—they don't eat much and they don't require a lot of specialized care. It's almost as easy to have two as it is to have one. Perhaps the largest extra expense you will have to consider is health care. Veterinary costs for checkups, vaccinations, and steriliza-tion surgery can be significant. Make sure you can afford double the costs before doubling your kitties!

PHYSICAL TRAITS: You might already have a picture of the cat of your dreams. Perhaps you want one with a perfect patchwork of calico spots or with fur so long you can bury your hand up to the wrist in softness. Before you become too enamored of certain physical traits, however, be sure to consider the practicality of certain feline features.

Physically, domestic cats have changed very little over the centuries, so they don't come in the great vari-ety of sizes and body types as dogs.

Yet, there seems to be more than enough variety in their colors and patterns to please just about everyone's desire for something different.

Although color is a benign personal choice, the length of hair it comes in is not. Long hair is always much more appealing in theory than in reality. If you don't invest the time to brush the fur frequently, the plush softness you hoped to enjoy will become marred with lumps of mats.

A lack of brushing will also result in globs of shed hair on your furniture and floors. So if you really love the beauty of long hair, be prepared to do the maintenance. Cats, by the way, are not fond of being shaved!

A number of mutations have become traits of certain cat breeds. Be aware that some of these characteristics may require higher maintenance from you. Or they may cause physical problems for the cat.

This longhaired cat will require more grooming to keep her coat clean and tangle-free. Be prepared for lots of fur around the house with a cat like this.

For example, hairless cats require protection from the sun and from temperature extremes. Persian-type cats with flattened noses can suffer breathing difficulties. You can choose any cat you want, but do so with open eyes.

TEMPERAMENTAL TRAITS: If you want to cuddle with a cat on a cold winter night, you need to find one that is just as crazy about cuddling as you are. If you want to be entertained by the monkey-like escapades of a kitty comedian, you need to find a spirited feline that loves the attention of an audience. And if you want a cat to provide companionship for another feline family member, you'll need to find an amiable and adaptable kitty that is receptive to companionship.

You can judge the temperament of an adult cat by spending a little bit of time with it. You might be surprised to discover the cat you "fell in love with at first sight" has no desire to be the lap kitty you really want. The cat you looked forward to caressing may be more interested in playing than being petted. So think about the

KITTY CAT PERSONALITIES

If your mixed breed cat physically resembles any of the following breeds, she may also have inherited some of that breed's personality traits:

Siamese, **Balinese**, and **Javanese** cats form a very close bond with humans. They can also be very vocal cats, whose "talking" can be hard to ignore.

Maine Coons are the teddy bears of the cat world. These large cats offer plenty of bulk to hug. They have loving, laid-back personalities that make them excellent family pets.

Persians are the epitome of lap cats, relishing every opportunity to lounge with and be spoiled by their owners.

Ragamuffins have an amazingly patient and tolerant temperament that makes them great family companions. They can be so relaxed as to become as limp as a rag in your arms. But they also have plenty of spirit for play.

Ragdolls are playful felines that appreciate a lot of human attention. For the most part, they are quiet and easygoing.

Russian Blues are exceptionally loyal and affectionate to their owners, although they can be a bit shy of strangers.

reasons you want a cat, and don't settle for less than what you want. You'll be much happier with your choice if you are choosy to begin with.

It's a little more difficult to evaluate the temperament of kittens, as they typically act very much alike—playful, inquisitive, and often a little wild. Sometimes cat personalities seem to be based more on chance than genetics. Kittens from the same litter can grow up to have vastly different personalities. Just be aware that kittens go through developmental phases. Their likes, dislikes, and behaviors change as they grow. They may be nice lap kitties as kittens, but then decide they'd rather lie beside you instead of on you when they reach adulthood. Mixed breed kittens do not come with temperament guarantees.

HEALTH: Finding the right cat mostly involves making choices about the traits you like and the characteristics that will fit the best into your lifestyle. But there is no decision to make when it comes to the health of your cat. Any feline you bring into your life should be healthy.

Never adopt an unhealthy-looking cat out of pity. You won't know how serious her medical issues are until a veterinarian has examined the cat.

Are the kittens wheezing? Do they have weepy eyes, nasal discharge, bloated belly, hair loss, flaky skin, or dull coats? Any sign of illness is your signal to look elsewhere for a cat companion. If just one kitten in a litter appears to be sick, the rest of the litter may be ill, too. Don't allow yourself to take a sickly pet home out of pity. The veterinary bills you may incur could be astronomical. And if you lose your new kitten, the price of your broken heart is incalculable.

CHOOSING A VETERINARIAN

It's not always easy to tell if a prospective pet is healthy just by looking at it. That's why it's important to have your new pet examined by a veterinarian as soon as possible. But you shouldn't take your new kitty to just any veterinarian—you need to take her to someone you trust.

If you don't already do business with a particular veterinarian, get referrals from friends and relatives, or contact veterinary hospitals listed in the phone book. Some of the things you need to consider are:

Is the veterinary hospital close enough to handle any emergencies you may encounter? You don't want to drive 10 miles to get to the clinic if your cat is choking or bleeding profusely.

Is the veterinarian a feline practitioner? This may or may not be important to you. If you have other pets, you may prefer a vet who can minister to all of your pets. But if cats are your only animal companions, you may prefer a feline specialty practice. It offers special expertise in feline health and amenities such as a quiet waiting room with no barking dogs.

Does the veterinarian charge competitive rates for exams, office charges, vaccinations, and neutering

Do the research before choosing a veterinarian. Finding a professional who is qualified, friendly, and knowledgeable will help keep your cat healthy for many years.

or spaying? Contact several veterinary hospitals in your area to find out the going rates for these services.

What kind of diagnostic, surgical, and laboratory equipment does the hospital possess? More services often mean higher veterinary fees, but they can also mean more convenience. Do you want to wait to get laboratory results? Do you mind being referred to another facility if your pet needs an ultrasound or other specialized diagnostic procedure?

Are the hospital's hours of operation convenient? If you have to take time off work every time your pet needs to see the vet, you may want to do business elsewhere.

Once you've found a veterinarian who appears to meet your expectations, you still need time to build trust with him. Always be observant of the kind of care and treatment you and your pet receive. Your veterinarian should take time to answer your questions in terms you can understand. The entire hospital staff should treat you and your cat with kindness and respect. When you are consistently impressed with the level of professionalism and service you receive, your veterinarian will become a valuable ally in keeping your cherished feline healthy.

❧❧❧

Providing the best possible beginning for your cat is a small investment that pays huge dividends. There is more than a little luck involved in finding the right cat to be your feline kindred spirit. It pays to choose your friends—even the animal ones—wisely!

CHAPTER FOUR

Caring for Your Cat

The more time and effort you put into caring for your pet, the greater benefits you will reap from it. Studies have shown that, aside from contributing to a strong bond between you and your cat, caring for pets is good for the physical and emotional well-being of humans.

PREPARING FOR YOUR CAT

There are many advantages to preparing for your cat before you bring her home. Taking care of arrangements ahead of time will help you avoid a lot of needless stress and frustration. It will help you avoid household conflicts and arguments. And most importantly, it will help prevent accidents or injuries to your new feline housemate.

SUPPLIES: There's a lot to think about when shopping for your cat's supplies. What kind of kitty toys do

Though your cat may find napping spots all over the house, make sure to get her a bed of her own and place it in a spot where she can observe all that's going on around her.

you think she'll like? What kind of treats will inspire her to come running when you call her name? You can choose a kitty bed to match the living room carpet and a collar to contrast with your kitty's fur color if you want. But you also want to keep some practical suggestions in mind.

When it comes to kitty beds, choose something washable, which allows for easy maintenance. And if you want your cat to actually use the bed, place it somewhere high, with a good view. Cats feel safe at a higher elevation. And they love watching everything going on around them.

Pet dishes, like many cat products, come in all kinds of fancy materials and designs. But keep your kitty's preferences in mind, too. A lot of people make the mistake of thinking a small cat should have small dishes. Cats, however, are not fond of having their whisker feelers smashed against the side of a small dish while eating or drinking. Larger, low-sided dishes are best for the tactilely sensitive domestic cat.

Make your job as kitty caretaker easier by getting dishes that are dishwasher safe and nonporous. Chose steel or porcelain bowls, as plastic is

Your cat's food and water dish should be wide, flat, and low to the ground, allowing plenty of room for her whiskers and nose.

more likely to harbor bacteria. If your kitty likes to push her dishes around, you might want to invest in heavier dishes. Or buy ones that are designed to be tip-free or splash-free.

Two items that require great care in their selection are the litter box and scratching post. Due to their important functions, these items must appeal to your cat. The "bigger is better" rule applies to both. A litter box should be at least 22 inches x 16 inches (56 x 41 cm) and a scratching post should be a minimum of 30 inches (76 cm) tall. Some cats are not comfortable using a small litter box, and a short scratching post may not be tall enough to allow your cat to get a good "stretch" when she scratches it. She may choose to use your furniture instead.

Another rule that applies to both these items is the "two is better than one." It is best to provide one litter box per cat, plus one. If, for any reason, your cat does not want to use one of the litter boxes, she will then have an alternate choice. Scratching posts, too, provide better protection against claw damage when there is more than one to choose from and they are strategically placed in prominent locations. Posts covered with sisal fabric or sisal rope are the most attractive to cats.

IDENTIFICATION: One of the most important items you will have to obtain for your cat is some form of identification. A collar with an I.D. tag is the most recognizable form of identification, but it does have some drawbacks. Cats are notorious for getting into difficult situations, including getting their collars caught on things. To avoid possible strangulation, you should always use a collar that is elasticized or has a breakaway feature so your cat can wiggle out of it.

Unfortunately, in attempting to keep your cat safe, you will also be making it easy for your pet to lose her identification. Some cats become so proficient at slipping out of collars, it's impossible to keep a collar on them. That's why it's important to have your cat microchipped.

A microchip is tiny capsule that can be injected under the skin, between your cat's shoulder blades. It contains a miniscule data chip that can be detected with a scanner. Most

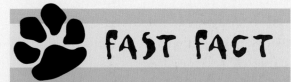

FAST FACT

Cats tend to prefer food at room temperature or warmer, the same temperature as freshly killed prey.

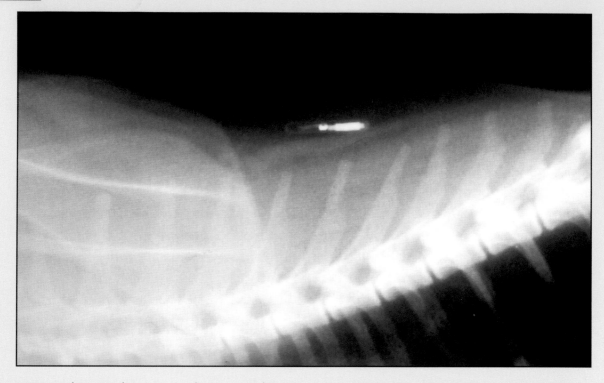

A microchip can be seen in this X-ray of a cat's spine. Microchipping your cat can increase the chances of finding her after she has been lost.

animal shelters and veterinarians are diligent about checking for microchips in lost cats. No cat should be without a microchip, which can be obtained through your veterinarian or an animal shelter.

KITTY PROOFING YOUR HOME

The cat's curious mind is one of its most endearing qualities. It's also an indication of the deep caverns of feline intelligence. By exploring, playing with, and testing the environment around them, cats learn many interesting aspects of life. Don't be surprised if your keen little kitty becomes self-taught in the art of opening things, like doors, cabinets, and drawers!

There are times, though, when a cat's experiments go wrong. You don't want your new cat to taste test electrical cords or consume something hazardous. You don't want your kitty to get her tail caught in a self-closing door that she just learned to open or get stuck behind your stove or refrigerator.

You need to kitty proof your home by blocking off dangerous areas and removing or covering hazardous items. Evaluate your home

FAST FACT

The importance of keeping some form of identification on your cat is illustrated by this sad fact: Only 4 percent of lost cats are ever reunited with their owners by U.S. animal shelters.

for safety, starting at floor level, just as you would if you had a baby in your home. But with a cat, you also need to evaluate higher spaces. Check the end tables, bookcases, and anywhere else your nimble feline may like to perch.

Since it's impossible to remove every single potential source of danger, you should supervise your new cat very closely for the first few weeks. That way you can see what kinds of hazardous items she is drawn to, and then take appropriate steps to prevent her access to those items. Kittens especially require vigilant supervision. When you are unable to watch her, you may want to confine your kitten to a safe room or pen.

Cats and kittens are particularly drawn to stringy and dangly objects, which pose a risk of strangulation. Worse, many cats can suffer life-threatening intestinal blockages from ingesting such items. It's important to keep yarn, string, streamers, and tinsel out of your cat's reach, and to put stringed kitty toys away when they are not being used.

HANDLING YOUR CAT

Some cats are much more tolerant of handling than others. Some don't mind being carried around like little babies. Others prefer not to be touched. Most cats use their very sharp claws and teeth to communicate their displeasure at being handled in ways they do not appreciate.

Keep a close watch on your kitty when she's playing with strings or yarn to ensure she doesn't eat them.

COMMON PLANTS POISONOUS TO CATS

Aloe vera	Hyacinth	Poinsettia
Chrysanthemum	Hydrangea	Poppy
Clematis	Lily	Potato
Crocus	Mistletoe	Rhododendron
Daffodil	Monkshood	Rhubarb
Foxglove	Morning glory	Tulip
Garlic	Oleander	Yew
Holly	Philodendron	

For a complete list, see the American Society for the Prevention of Cruelty to Animals (ASPCA) Animal Poison Control Center Web site at www.aspca.org.

It is very important to respect your particular cat's preferences.

Still, it's important for your cat to tolerate a certain level of handling so that you (and your veterinarian) can take proper care of her. It's not realistic or productive to try to force your cat to lie quietly in your arms for hours on end. But you can teach your cat to allow some handling with a minimum of fuss. This can be accomplished by picking your cat or kitten up occasionally and giving her a treat while you are holding her. Frequent grooming and claw trimming will also help your cat get used to being handled.

Regardless of how tolerant they are, cats should never be picked up by the scruff of the neck. Even though mother cats pick up and carry their kittens this way, it is not an appropriate method for humans to use. It is recommended only when needed as a method of restraint. The best way to pick up your cat is by putting one hand underneath her body, just behind the front legs. Then use your other hand to scoop under and support her hindquarters. Your kitty will feel most secure if you hold her close to your body.

Even when your cat is the one who initiates physical contact, always be observant of the terms she lays out for you. If she keeps trying to climb onto your shoulder, you might find that she enjoys riding there! If your cat lies in your lap facing away from you, she may want to enjoy the warm contact without being petted. If she lies in your lap facing toward you, she may be more receptive to attention and petting.

RULES FOR CHILDREN

Children may not have the strength, coordination, or maturity to handle a cat properly. They may not be responsible enough to make sure all of a cat's needs are met. They may not recognize unsafe situations. All of these concerns point to the necessity of establishing rules and expectations so that children can enjoy having a feline pet—without compromising safety or health for either of them.

Of course, children should be taught to respect their cat. They should learn to not pull on her tail, poke her eyes, tease her, or dress her in doll clothes for a tea party (unless the cat actually likes it). Here are some questions to think about in establishing rules:

Who will be responsible for your cat's care? Who will feed her? Who will clean her litter box? How often and when will these duties be done?

What restrictions will be applied to handling? Young children should not be allowed to pick up or hold a cat without supervision and guidance.

Do you need to restrict play time so your kitty can get a cat nap once in awhile? Do you need to provide an area off-limits to children so your kitty can have a "safe zone" away from them?

The ultimate responsibility for a pet's welfare lies with the adults in the home. Owning a cat can provide an excellent opportunity for parents to teach kids how to be responsible for a pet. But adults should be prepared to take over the kitty care

Pet ownership is a great way to teach children responsibility. However, an adult must supervise to make sure the cat is receiving proper care.

duties if it becomes too difficult to get the children to do them. No cat should be relinquished to an animal shelter just because the novelty of having a pet wore off.

INTRODUCING OTHER PETS

Observing two animals communicate with each other, especially when they are different species, can be fascinating. Animals tend to converse in a simple language that indicates what they like, what they don't like, and what they don't care about. When animals listen to each other and respect each other's feelings, they get along wonderfully. You can assist your pets in developing such a relationship by introducing them properly.

Slow is the way to go. Keep your pets separated by using barriers—doors or door gates—in the beginning. This allows the animals to adjust to each other's presence. When your new cat seems comfortable in her environment, and your other pets seem to accept the new arrival, you can attempt to introduce your pets face-to-face. Allow your pets to see, hear, and smell each other without coming into contact. If you have a dog, you will have better control if you keep him on a leash during the introduction process.

Even if your pets do not become best buddies, they may learn to tolerate each other. The key to success is to afford each animal his or her own space. Your new kitty may need a perch that will allow her to escape the overzealous attention of your dog or resident cat. The newcomer shouldn't have to worry about competing for food. And don't forget to give your existing pets plenty of attention. They

If introduced in the proper way, a cat and dog can become fast friends.

were here first. Avoid any problems with jealousy, by giving them their privilege of seniority.

FEEDING

Manufacturers of commercially prepared cat foods have made it easy for cat owners to provide a balanced diet for their feline friends. Most commercial cat foods meet the Association of American Feed Control Officials (AAFCO) minimum requirements as complete and balanced. However, "balanced" does not necessarily mean "nutritious." How do you know which cat foods are quality products and which ones are not? And what difference does it really make?

Your cat's diet has a direct and very noticeable effect on your cat's health and appearance. Investing in a good diet now can save you hundreds of dollars in veterinary bills later. Your cat's attitude, energy level, immunity, coat quality, and even longevity are all related to what she eats.

To determine which foods provide quality nutrition, simply check the ingredients. If the first ingredient is meat—such as chicken, beef or fish—you're on the right track. Cats are strict carnivores (unlike dogs, which are omnivores), so meat is the most important part of their diet. If the first item on an ingredient list is grain, rice, or a

AVOID HAVING A FAT CAT!

The fattest cat on record was a male tabby named Himmy from Queensland, Australia. He weighed almost 47 pounds (21 kg)! The *Guinness Book of World Records* has since stopped accepting entries for this record to avoid encouraging the purposeful overfeeding of cats.

If you don't want your cat to compete with this record, adhere to the following good feeding practices:

- Feed at regular times each day.
- Provide fresh water daily.
- Keep food and water bowls clean.
- Provide a good quality cat or kitten food.

- Measure the amount of food and adjust the amount according to your cat's weight.
- Avoid feeding "people food" to your cat, and limit the amount of treats.

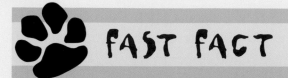

FAST FACT

Many modern pet owners have embraced the trend of alternative diets for pets, such as raw food diets and home-cooked diets. Never implement these types of diets without thoroughly researching them to ensure you are providing nutritionally balanced meals. And keep in mind that cats are strict carnivores. Vegetarian diets for cats are not only unhealthy; they are cruel.

meat byproduct, this is a sign of lower quality cat food.

For good skin and coat condition, your cat needs a source of omega-3 and omega-6 fatty acids. Quality sources include fish oil or flaxseed oil. The ingredient list will also indicate what type of preservative is used. Vitamin E and C are natural preservatives, often listed as "mixed tocopherols." They are safer and healthier than artificial preservatives such as butylated hydroxyanisole

(BHA), butylated hydroxytoluene (BHT), or ethoxyquin.

The assumption that cats are finicky eaters is unwarranted. Cats may have individual preferences when it comes to certain flavors, but overall, cats prefer whatever they have been typically fed. So if you get in the habit of feeding your cat high-priced gourmet foods, you can expect your cat to prefer or even demand that kind of food.

The most practical diet for your cat is a combination of both dry and canned foods. Although canned foods are more expensive, cats typically prefer the more natural texture and flavor of wet foods from cans. The additional moisture content is also good for them.

GROOMING

Cats are such beautiful creatures because they take such good care of themselves. Shorthaired cats in particular always seem to be perfectly fluffed and fuzzy. You will rarely see a cat with a flaky or oily coat, or with clumps of shed hair tarnishing its sleek appearance—unless it is sick.

Pay attention to the ingredients listed on your cat's food packaging. Be sure only premium grade foods are included.

FAST FACT

For reasons that are believed to be genetic, some cats react intensely to catnip, but some do not. Similarly, some cats absolutely love to chase a laser pointer beam, while others are not at all interested.

BATHING: Cats maintain their immaculate coats by frequently grooming themselves. Their abrasive tongues function as both combs and bathing apparatus. For this reason,

Most of the time, cats will clean their coats themselves. If you do need to bathe your kitty, hold her firmly but gently, and talk in a soothing voice to reassure her that a bath is safe.

cats rarely need their owners to give them baths. However, a cat may happen to get into something oily or sticky, or need a bath for some other reason. When giving a cat a bath, keep the following in mind:

First, keep things safe. Cats are not known to be fond of baths. While bathing your cat, keep one hand on her at all times. A rubber mat or towel on the bottom of the sink can help prevent the animal from slipping.

Second, use the right bathing products. Cats are very sensitive to scents. You should use a very mild pet shampoo—preferably one made exclusively for cats. Wash your cat's face only if it is absolutely necessary, and be sure to use a tearless shampoo if you do.

Third, most cats prefer to air dry. Keep your cat in a warm environment until she is thoroughly dry. If you have a longhaired cat that needs some drying assistance, use a hair dryer on a low heat, low velocity setting.

BRUSHING: Some cats can live their entire lives without ever requiring a bath. Most can get by without being brushed, too, but there are many benefits to regularly brushing your cat. It can help prevent or reduce the incidence of hairballs—those wads of hair that accumulate over time in a cat's stomach from self-grooming. Brushing can also reduce the amount of shed hair in your home. But more importantly, brushing simply feels good. To your cat, it is like getting a luxurious back scratch or a relaxing massage. It can be a pleasurable bonding activity for you, too.

Regular brushing is a necessity for longhaired cats, which are much more prone to hairballs and mats. While some people think it is hard to keep up with this chore, the time commitment is only a few minutes per week. Make brushing your cat a

A slicker brush will remove loose fur from your cat's undercoat. Regular brushing will reduce the amount of shed fur in your home.

part of your regular routine by doing it on the same day of the week and at the same time.

Using the proper grooming tools will make the job easier. Shorthaired cats love the soothing massage of rubber curry brushes. Longhaired cats benefit more from the penetrating effects of cat slicker brushes. These thin wire tines have blunted tips that prevent scratching the cat's delicate skin. You may have to experiment with different products to find one that pleases your particular feline.

NAIL CARE

Trimming your cat's nails minimizes damage to your furniture if your cat is not trained to use a scratching post. And it can also prevent injuries to you and your cat. If your cat's nails are getting snagged on furnishings, or her talon-like claws are penetrating your clothes, it's probably time to give your kitty a manicure. Most cats will require a nail trim about every three to four weeks.

Nail trimming is a relatively simple process that can be done with a human toenail clipper or, if you have a very large cat, with a small animal nail clipper. Gently squeeze the toes of the paw so that the claws descend from their sheaths. The claws are translucent, so it's easy to see the quick, which provides the blood supply to the nail. As you trim the nail, avoid cutting into the quick, as this will cause your cat pain. If you do nick the blood vessel, you can use a styptic pencil or blood coagulant powders to quickly stop the bleeding. These items are available at pet supply stores; purchase some and keep it on hand, just in case.

Of course, an uncooperative kitty can make this relatively easy procedure difficult, and make cutting the quick more likely. When it comes to a battle of wills between humans and cats, cats usually win. So don't fight with your feline. Wait until your cat is in a calm mood before attempting to trim her nails. Don't feel bad about waking her up from her nap to do it. She'll be much more obliging.

It helps to get cats used to having their nails trimmed when they are kittens. However, even adult cats will adjust to nail trimming when it is done on a regular basis. If you are squeamish about trimming your cat's nails, ask your veterinarian or a professional pet groomer to assist you until you gain the confidence to do it yourself.

DENTAL CARE: Due to the incidence of dental disease in cats and dogs, more attention has been paid in the past decade to dental care for pets. The teeth of carnivores living in the

Trimming a cat's nails can be a trying task. To prevent injury to your cat, make sure she's relaxed and proceed with patience and caution.

wild are healthy because they eat the fibrous tissues of freshly killed meat and chew on abrasive bones. The commercial foods fed to pets tend to stick to their teeth and cause dental problems.

To prevent dental disease in your cat, brush her teeth once a week. You can use one of a number of pet dental products on the market. If you introduce dental care gradually and keep it brief, both kittens and adult cats will learn to accept it. Be sure to give plenty of praise and treats when your cat shows her willingness to tolerate the procedure. Like nail trimming, it helps to work with your cat when she is in a calm mood.

GROOMING AS A HEALTH CHECK

Taking care of your cat's hygienic needs makes it easy for you to keep abreast of your cat's health and condition. Every time you groom or handle your pet, you have the opportunity to discover injuries, lumps, sore spots, or symptoms of illness. You might even realize your cat is gaining or losing weight, or perhaps acting oddly.

Regular grooming, therefore, should be conducted as a health check for your pet. When you detect health problems early, you increase the likelihood of a favorable outcome for your cat. Regular grooming will also make your cat more tolerant of handling, something that provides advantages at home and at the vet's office.

≈≈≈≈

Caring for your cat should not be done because it is "necessary." It should be the whole purpose of owning a cat! You'll get the most out of cat ownership if you genuinely enjoy meeting the needs of your kitty companion.

CHAPTER FIVE

Training and Activities

Cats have an undeserved reputation of being untrainable. They may not have an innate desire to please humans as dogs do, but this does not mean cats can't be trained. The truth is that your cat must be trained in order to live harmoniously in your household. She needs to be trained to use a litter box and scratching post. She needs to learn household manners, such as staying off kitchen counters and not chewing on TV

Cats are intelligent and can be trained to obey household rules.

cords. She needs to learn to play nice without biting and scratching people.

TRAINING

Because the cat has extraordinary intelligence, she is actually well suited for training. She displays her genius every time she wants something, such as finding a way to open a door or getting to a hard-to-reach sunny spot. And so, the trick to training your cat is to convince your cat that she wants the same things you do!

LITTER BOX TRAINING TIPS:
According to the nonprofit educational organization Cats International, pet owners cite "the failure to use the litter box" as the most common complaint about their cat's behavior. Cats will almost always prefer to use a litter box rather than soil their homes. Because they have a very strong natural instinct to bury their waste, a litter box is the ideal solution. When a cat doesn't use its litter box, there is a reason. To avoid litter box lapses, you need to eliminate any reasons your cat has for shunning the litter box. Here are some tips for making use of the litter box attractive to your cat:

- Always provide more than one litter box. Some cats like to use one for urinating and one for defecat-

ing. If you have more than one cat, provide one litter box per cat, plus one extra litter box. This will provide an option in case one is already occupied, or if a territorial cat insists on having her own private facilities.

- Make sure your cat is neutered or spayed. Intact males are known to mark their territory with urine. Intact females in heat will urinate about the house to "advertise" their sexual state.

- Clean the litter boxes frequently. Most cats are content with a weekly cleaning, but some are very fussy about having a clean toilet.

- Location is important. Cats prefer a quiet, private place to do their business. Each litter box should have its own separate location.

There are dozens of brands of litter boxes on the market. Some are small, some are large, some are self-cleaning, and some match the furniture. Just remember that it is important to get one that your cat likes, so she'll use it. When choosing a box, consider the following:

Some cats can be quite persnickety about their litter box. Avoid purchasing litter boxes with covers—the

When training a kitten, an uncovered litter box works best. She'll be able to see the litter more easily. The litter box should be placed in an out-of-the-way area, but one that your cat can easily access. If you have more than one cat, each will probably need her own litter box.

confined quarters and the smell inside them can be disagreeable to some cats. And don't use litter box liners, which cats can find annoying. A simple rectangular litter box with a minimum size of 22 inches x 16 inches is often the best and most economical choice.

Don't forget that cats can be very sensitive to scents, so it is best to avoid using scented litter material. Don't use deodorizers or perfumes, either. And be careful not to use harsh cleaning chemicals to clean the litter box. An adequate litter box cleaning schedule will make the use of such products unnecessary.

SCRATCHING POST TRAINING: Cats are genetically programmed to scratch on vertical objects. This is how they shed the husks of their claws to sharpen them. It's how they mark their territory with scratch marks and scent. And it's how they get a good stretch now and then. As many cat owners have discovered, the corners of couches are ideal for these purposes.

If you want to train your cat to use a scratching post instead of your couch, you need to provide a more attractive alternative. The ideal scratching post must meet several requirements. The post needs

LITTER BOX AVERSION

Failure to use the litter box is the most common feline behavioral problem. Here are some causes:

- The cat is suffering from a health condition.
- The cat is not neutered or spayed.
- The litter box is not kept clean.
- The litter box is not in a quiet area.
- The litter box has a hood or plastic liners.
- The litter is scented or the box was washed with a harsh cleaning product.
- There are not enough litter boxes in the house, or they are all in the same area.
- There are territory disputes over the litter box among household cats.
- The cat is stressed by changes in its environment or routine.

to be at least 30 inches high because that provides a tall enough reach for your cat's morning stretch. It should be solid and sturdy enough for your cat to climb on it if she desires. A kitty that likes to sit on the top of the world would espe-

cially relish a scratching post with a perch on top.

The post should be covered with material that allows for maximum claw penetration. Cats like rough materials, such as coarse fabrics, sisal rope, or wood. These surfaces allow them to sink their claws in and get some resistance. Most carpet-covered posts fall short in this regard. Get your kitty something that provides satisfactory clawing.

In order to sufficiently advertise her presence with scent and scratch marks, your cat needs to have her scratching post in a prominent location, where everyone can see it. If she has already begun to target a piece of furniture, park the post in front of it. You can make the scratching post even more appealing by rubbing catnip on it. Then, praise your cat lavishly every time she uses the post.

It's better to have more than one scratching post. Give your kitty a choice of posts with different scratching materials, and put them in different locations. In most cases, your clawing kitty will leave the couch alone. But if she continues to use the furniture, you can make the couch less attractive for clawing. Simply apply double-sided tape and clear contact paper to the sofa corners, making the surface sticky or smooth. This will help

Kitty scratching posts can range from simple to complex, such as the "cat condo" pictured here. These playthings feature scratching surfaces, toys, and a tall perch area so your cat can survey her surroundings.

redirect your cat to her scratching posts, and she will get in the habit of scratching on the appropriate object.

PROBLEM BEHAVIORS

You can't blame a cat for being a cat. Cats don't see anything wrong with using their teeth and claws when they play. Their instincts do not include a desire to stay off the counters or dinner table. And their biological clock tells them it's perfectly acceptable to play at all hours of the night.

When you invite a cat to live with you, you assume responsibility for teaching your cat the rules of the house. But first, you should be aware of the rules of training. You

FAST FACT

Cats do not engage in undesirable behavior to "get even" with their owners. Cats behave in ways that are influenced by instinct and environmental factors.

must never physically discipline your cat. This will do absolutely no good, and it may do plenty of harm. It's not fair or effective to punish a cat for being a cat.

When your cat engages in behavior you find undesirable, try to redirect her to a more appropriate activity whenever possible. Be patient and consistent. And when your cat responds correctly, be very generous with praise, petting, or food rewards.

ROUGH PLAY: Do not use your hands when playing with your cat or kitten. Cats can become over-excited and give you some nasty scratches. If your cat rolls onto her side or back when you try to pet her, she's trying to tell you she's in the mood for playing, not petting. Get a toy and let her expend her energy in an appropriate way.

If your cat or kitten persistently attacks your hands, legs, or feet, you need to immediately indicate your displeasure. Then try to redirect her to another activity. Sometimes cats get a little too wild and need a "time out" to settle down. Whenever this happens, stop playing with your cat for a few minutes until she can regain some self-control. If you are consistent with these methods, your cat will soon learn the rules of fair play.

AGGRESSION: When cats show aggression towards people or other animals, it can be a very serious problem—one that requires expert advice. Do not hesitate to contact your veterinarian, an animal behaviorist, or a nonprofit animal welfare organization to seek solutions to aggression issues.

There are some situations, however, that you may be able to remedy yourself. Many cases of cat aggression are related to stress. If you can determine the source of your cat's stress and remove it, you can turn your combative kitty into a peaceable cat.

FAST FACT

To communicate effectively with your cat, you should develop and consistently use various vocal cues. First, decide how you will indicate your displeasure. A distinctive, sharp sound works best, such as "shhht" or "uh-uh." Likewise, you can choose a word or sound to indicate your pleasure, like a soft cluck or kissing sound. Also, decide what word or sound you will use to call your cat. Will you say, "Here, kitty, kitty," or call her by name? All these cues should be delivered consistently in the same tone of voice. Your cat will soon learn what they mean and how to respond to them.

For instance, some cats can become quite upset when they see another cat outside, roaming near their home territory. Because they can't get at the cat to chase it off, they may redirect their aggression to people or animals in the home. There are two things you can do to diffuse your feline's fury: Pull the curtains or shades shut so your cat can't see the intruder. And use a pheromone spray to help calm your irate kitty. Feline pheromone sprays contain hormones that can calm kitties in many stressful situations, including trips to the vet, adjusting to another cat, or adjusting to a new home. The sprays are available in pet supply stores.

Keeping a spray bottle on hand is a good way to show kitty where she is not permitted.

OFF-LIMIT AREAS: It's probably not a good practice to allow your kitty on the kitchen counters or tables. With its hot stove burners and sharp knives, a kitchen can be a dangerous place. And it's also not very appetizing to get kitty hair in your food. If your cat jumps up on the counter, shoo her off by clapping your hands and issuing a displeasure cue, like "shht!" or "uh uh!" If necessary, a squirt from a water-filled spray bottle is a good deterrent.

There are a number of effective deterrents you can use to keep kitty off your counters when you aren't home. Pieces of carpet runners facing point-side up are prickly to sensitive kitty paws. Or you can purchase a motion-detecting device made especially for cats that emits a burst of hissing air, a sound that cats hate.

Do you need to discourage your cat from playing with the cords behind your computer? To repel her from the area, use your cat's olfactory sensitivities to your advantage by putting an air freshener or bar of scented soap there. Cats are very responsive to these types of "remote" or environmental corrections. Best of all, most cats can be trained so that

LEASH TRAINING

To give your cat opportunities to explore the outdoors, consider leash training. While your cat is on a leash, be sure to supervise to make sure she doesn't get tangled in it.

1. The first step in leash training is to get your kitty accustomed to wearing a collar. Harness-type collars are the safest and most secure. Put the collar on the cat and have her wear it around the house for a few days so she can get used to it.

2. Next, hook a light leash to her collar and let it drag behind her. The leash may annoy her at first, but she'll soon begin to ignore it. An offering of treats is a good distraction!

3. Finally, start adding some light resistance to the leash so your cat can get used to the restriction. Gradually add more resistance until she learns to accept the limits of her leash. Then, it's time to get some fresh air!

the use of deterrents can eventually be discontinued.

NOCTURNAL DISTURBANCES: Cats aren't really nocturnal animals. They are considered crepuscular, which means they are most active at dusk and dawn. Still, it's not unusual for cats to stay up a little too late or get up a little too early. If your feisty feline is intruding on your sleep, you can encourage her to keep better playtime hours.

First, make sure your cat gets some exercise at least an hour before bedtime. Unless she's tired it can be hard for her to sleep. To help her feel drowsy, give her a good meal in the evening. Many behavior issues can be solved by managing and manipulating a cat's feeding schedule, exercise schedule, and environment.

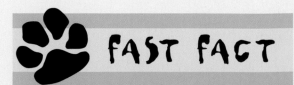

FAST FACT

Does your indoor-only cat yowl incessantly to go outside? Some cats just aren't happy as indoor-only pets. If your cat is one of them, let her out safely by providing a secure outdoor enclosure.

ACTIVITIES

While it's fun to simply play with your cat, there are other activities you can do, especially if your cat has an outgoing, friendly personality. You might consider showing your cat, participating in feline agility competitions, or doing volunteer therapy work. All of these activities are great ways to share your special feline with others.

SHOWING YOUR MIXED BREED CAT: You don't have to own a pedigreed cat to compete at cat shows. Your mixed breed charmer can win awards and ribbons, just like the fancy pedigreed cats! Showing your cat can be a fun and rewarding hobby, especially if you have a cat that likes the excitement and attention as much as you.

A number of cat clubs offer Household Pet classes for cats without pedigrees. Check with various clubs to see if your cat meets the requirements for this class. The Cat Fanciers' Association requires non-pedigreed cats to be neutered or spayed if they are over eight months old, and they may not be declawed. The International Cat Association, on the other hand, will allow declawed cats, as well as cats with physical handicaps.

Mixed breed cats are judged on their condition, temperament, and unique physical features. Does your cat have the right charisma? Even if your particular cat finds the show experience too stressful, you don't need to show your cat in order to enjoy attending cat shows.

CAT AGILITY COMPETITIONS: Cat shows aren't just for showing off a cat's pleasing appearance. Many shows also offer cat agility competitions in which cats earn titles by

If your cat is particularly good at navigating her way through tight spots, perhaps she might be good at agility competition!

being the best in traversing an obstacle course. Obstacles may consist of jumps, tunnels, and other items set up within a securely fenced area. Cats are coaxed through the course by their owners, usually by using a cat teaser.

For the cats, it's all about play. For their owners, it's all about fun. And for the spectators, it's all about admiring the athletic abilities of the competing felines. Your pet will need practice and training so that she feels comfortable participating in this sport. But this is mainly accomplished by simply playing with your cat—a lot! For more information about this fun new hobby for housecat owners, visit the International Cat Agility Tournaments Web site.

THERAPY CAT: Therapy animals visit nursing homes, schools, and other institutions to bring love and companionship to people. Although therapy work is often associated with dogs, there are many different kinds of therapy animals. They include rabbits, Guinea pigs, parrots—and cats!

A therapy cat needs to have an extremely gentle personality and must enjoy human contact. Feline "therapists" must also be comfortable in new environments and be able to tolerate vehicle travel.

If you think your cat has what it takes to be a therapy cat, you can get started by contacting a local pet therapy organization. To find listings of organizations in your area, visit the Therapy Dog International Web site. You can also find information, instruction, and support at the Web site for the Delta Society, which features a Pet Partner program.

TRAVELING WITH YOUR CAT

Some adventuresome cats tend to be receptive to the idea of exploring the world from the window of a motorhome. However, more reclusive ones prefer to never put a paw in any type of moving vehicle. Regardless of how your cat feels about travel, there are times when you have to take her for a ride—to visit the vet or move to a new home, for example. Here are some suggestions that will make the trip a little more fun and a little less frustrating for both of you:

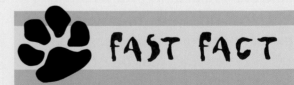

FAST FACT

If your cat hates being transported in a vehicle, drape a towel or blanket over her carrier to help keep her quiet. Be sure to leave the door uncovered to allow for air circulation.

A sturdy pet carrier is necessary when planning any kind of travel with your cat.

Make a list of all cat care items you need to pack, so you won't forget anything. Does your cat need any medications? Did you include some toys to keep her busy?

Always make sure your cat has some form of identification. Bring a current photo of your cat along with health information. Having this information will make it easier to find your pet if she gets lost.

Transport your cat in a pet carrier. If your cat has an aversion to vehicle travel, spray some pheromone spray in the carrier shortly before you leave, or ask your veterinarian about using sedatives.

Do not leave your cat unattended in a tightly closed vehicle. This is especially true in warmer climates. Be sure to crack a window and make sure there is enough air circulation to prevent your cat from becoming overheated.

WHEN YOU CAN'T BE THERE

If you decide to leave your kitty at home, you can provide for your pet's needs in other ways. Pet sitters and boarding establishments are both good options, depending on your situation.

PET SITTERS: Cats make great pets for people who travel. They are somewhat forgiving of their owners' brief absences. Unlike dogs, they won't chew up a living room ensemble out of loneliness or boredom, and they won't disturb neighbors by barking all night. The ease of caring for cats can make it easy to find someone willing to care for them when you're away. You can ask a trustworthy neighbor or friend to stop by a couple times a day to make sure the cat is fed, has her water replenished, and receives a few chin scratches. But if you will be gone for more than a couple days, you may want to hire a professional pet sitter.

The advantage of having a professional pet sitter is that he can take care of your home as well as your cat. You can ask the sitter to bring in the mail and newspapers, take care of houseplants, and take steps to prevent a burglary while you are gone.

Web sites like Petsitters.org are great places to start your search for a qualified cat-sitter.

Before hiring a pet sitter, be sure to interview him in person. A pet sitter should be knowledgeable about cats and show an interest in your special feline. People who are serious about the profession belong to one or more professional organizations, such as the National Association of Professional Pet Sitters (NAPPS) or Pet Sitters International (PSI). Check with these organizations for referrals to members in your area.

CAT BOARDING: An alternative to hiring a pet sitter is boarding your cat at a kennel or with a veterinarian. This is a less ideal situation as many cats become stressed from changes in their environment. They are also exposed to other animals, which increases their chances of contracting a contagious illness. However, you may find yourself in a situation in which you need to consider boarding.

Before checking your kitty into a kennel, do some research. Will she have her own accommodations? Does the kennel only have cats, or will there be a mix of other animals? There are no right answers, but you want to find a kennel where she'll feel comfortable and secure.

Some dog boarding kennels offer cat boarding services. If you chose this kind of kennel, make sure the cat area is isolated from the dog area. The noise and smell of nearby canines can be stressful for your cat. Your cat's accommodations should be clean, odor-free, and as spacious as possible.

A better situation might be to place your pet with a feline veterinarian who offers cat boarding services. The facility is likely to be much quieter for sensitive felines. In addition, having a veterinarian on call in case of an emergency is a fringe benefit.

⌘⌘⌘

Just because cats don't constantly ask for attention doesn't mean they don't want it. Whether or not you are interested in pursuing training or individual activities with your cat, you should spend as much time as you can with your pet. Play with her and talk to her constantly. You'll be amazed how she will respond to you!

CHAPTER SIX

Keeping Your Cat Healthy

The relationship you share with your feline is unique. You want to savor that experience as long as you possibly can. And there is no better way to do that than by keeping your cat happy and healthy for many years to come.

THE FIRST VET VISIT

Shortly after you acquire your new cat or kitten, she should be examined

One of your first tasks as a new cat owner will be to have the vet check your pet.

by a veterinarian. This checkup will tell you if your new feline companion has any preexisting health conditions. This exam is just the first of many checkups your pet will experience throughout her life. Cats should receive a regular checkup every year.

Be sure to prepare for your visit to the veterinarian. First, write down any questions you have about your cat's health or behavior, and bring this list with you to the checkup. Second, bring a stool sample from your pet so your veterinarian can check for internal parasites. During the visit, the veterinarian will check your cat from head to tail for any signs of illness or abnormality. He'll answer your questions and recommend appropriate vaccinations or procedures.

VACCINATIONS

Not all vaccinations are appropriate for all cats in all situations. This is why it is important to seek your veterinarian's advice. However, several viruses are highly dangerous or pose a serous threat to a large segment of the feline population. The vaccines for these viruses are recommended for all cats. These so-called core vaccines prevent diseases such as feline panleukopenia, feline viral respiratory disease complex, and rabies. All other feline vaccines are not considered core vaccines.

FELINE PANLEUKOPENIA (FPV): Also known as feline distemper, feline panleukopenia is common in cats less than a year old. Unfortunately, this viral disease is very often fatal to kittens. Signs of this illness include fever, listlessness, loss of appetite, vomiting, and diarrhea. FPV is a highly contagious disease that spreads through contact with an infected animal's secretions. Once infected, a cat requires prompt treatment, as FPV can kill quickly.

Your vet will know which vaccinations your cat will need.

VACCINATION SCHEDULE

This schedule is based on the current Feline Vaccination Guidelines issued by the American Association of Feline Practitioners:

Vaccines	Core	Kittens	Boosters
Panleukopenia Virus (FPV)	Yes	First dose at 6 to 8 weeks of age, and then every 3 to 4 weeks until 16 weeks old	1 year after initial series, and every 3 years thereafter
Feline Herpesvirus (FHV)	Yes	First dose at 6 to 8 weeks of age, and then every 3 to 4 weeks until 16 weeks old	1 year after initial series, and every 3 years thereafter
Feline Calicivirus (FCV)	Yes	First dose at 6 to 8 weeks of age, and then every 3 to 4 weeks until 16 weeks old	1 year after initial series, and every 3 years thereafter
Rabies	Yes	One dose at 8 to 12 weeks of age	Booster after 1 year and then annually or every 3 years, depending on vaccine
Feline Leukemia Virus (FeLV)	No	First dose at 8 to 12 weeks of age; second dose 3 to 4 weeks later	1 year after initial series, then annually thereafter for at-risk cats
Feline Immunodeficiency Virus (FIV)	No	First dose at 8 weeks of age; second and third doses at 2- to 3-week intervals	1 year after initial series, then annually thereafter for at-risk cats
Chlamydophila Felis	No	First dose at 9 weeks of age; second dose 3 to 4 weeks later	Annual boosters for at-risk cats
Bordetella Bronchiseptica	No	First intranasal dose at 8 weeks of age	Annual boosters for at-risk cats

Core vaccines are those recommended for all cats by the American Association of Feline Practitioners; other vaccines are given at the discretion of individual veterinarians. (Feline Infectious Peritonitis (FIP) and Feline Giardia vaccines are generally not recommended.)

Since almost all cats are exposed to this virus at some point in their lives, they must receive this vaccination.

FELINE VIRAL RESPIRATORY DISEASE: Viral respiratory disease is very common in cats. Initial symptoms of sneezing and discharge from the eyes and nose progress to more serious symptoms of fever, listlessness, and loss of appetite. Although not considered life-threatening for adult cats, the disease can be deadly for kittens.

There are two viruses in particular that are responsible for the great majority of respiratory infections: feline viral rhinotracheitis (FVR) and feline calicivirus (FCV). To prevent or lessen the effect of both of these viruses, veterinarians administer feline viral respiratory disease complex vaccine. This vaccine is often combined with the feline panleukopenia vaccine and given as a single inoculation.

RABIES: Rabies is a particularly devastating viral disease. Its victims suffer inflammation of the brain, and symptoms that include confusion and the inability to swallow. Infected animals often become aggressive and unpredictable. Worst of all, rabies is incurable and fatal. Because of the seriousness of this disease and the

fact that it can be transmitted to humans, you are required by law to vaccinate your cat against rabies. Your veterinarian can advise you of the rabies ordinance in effect in your area.

FELINE LEUKEMIA VIRUS (FELV): The feline leukemia virus, which suppresses the cat's immune system, can affect cats in very different ways. Some cats recover completely. Some never completely get rid of the virus. They remain contagious until they eventually succumb to FeLV-related diseases. There are also some cats that develop a long-lasting latent

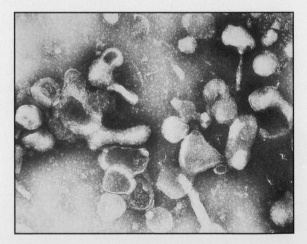

This image taken by an electron microscope shows the retrovirus Feline Leukemia Virus (FeLV). FeLV is a very common feline disease passed from one cat to another via adversarial bites, or when one cat sneezes on another, or shares a food bowl. A cat may be vaccinated in order to protect it from acquiring this virus, which is often fatal.

infection from which they may or may not recover.

The symptoms of FeLV, which may include fever, weight loss, vomiting, or diarrhea, mimic those of many other illnesses. Because of this, diagnosis is confirmed by a blood test. Since the disease is spread through repeated exposure to an infected cat, indoor cats that do not come in contact with other felines are at a very low risk of infection. Outdoor cats, however, face much greater risks, as they tend to fight over territory and can spread the disease through bites and scratches. Due to the potentially grim outlook for infected cats, vaccination is recommended for any at-risk felines.

FELINE INFECTIOUS PERITONITIS (FIP): Feline infectious peritonitis is triggered by a coronavirus that is common in cats. Most of them recover from the coronavirus—sometimes without ever showing the mild cold-like symptoms that accompany this disease. However, a small number of cats (less than 1 percent) will develop feline infectious peritonitis. There is some evidence that susceptibility to this disease is hereditary. It tends to affect cats under 2 years old and over 14 years old.

Symptoms of FIP may include listlessness, weight loss, or fluid retention in the chest or abdomen. This disease is fatal, although with proper management the eventual outcome may be postponed for several years. There is an intranasal (sprayed into the nose) vaccine available. However, due to the low risk most cats face and the limited effectiveness of the vaccine, it is not usually recommended.

BORDETELLA BRONCHISEPTICA: An intranasal vaccine is also available for *Bordetella bronchiseptica*, a bacterium that causes respiratory disease in cats. The infection results in cold-like symptoms, which are generally not considered serious. However, *B. bronchiseptica* can cause death in young kittens if the infection develops into bronchopneumonia. The bacteria are more prevalent in some areas than others, so the decision to vaccinate your cat depends on where you live, the age of your cat, and your cat's exposure to other felines. Your veterinarian is the best person to make vaccination recommendations.

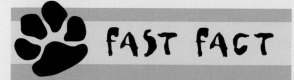

FAST FACT

Cats that have demodectic mange may also suffer from an immunosuppressive disease such as FeLV or FIV.

GIARDIA FELIS: *Giardia felis* is a protozoan parasite that lives in the intestinal tracts of cats and causes diarrhea. Infections can be treated with medications, and reinfection can be prevented with appropriate management practices such as disinfecting the environment. Like many feline diseases, *Giardia felis* infection is low risk for indoor-only cats that are not exposed to environments occupied by other cats. Use of the vaccine for this parasite is limited to situations where infection is a problem in a larger population of cats.

CHLAMYDOPHILA FELIS: The bacterium *Chlamydophila felis* causes respiratory disease in cats and is spread directly from cat to cat. The vaccine for *Chlamydophila felis* does not prevent illness, but it does lessen the severity of symptoms. Prevalence of the bacterium varies by location, and the vaccine is known to cause adverse reactions in a small percentage of cats. For these reasons, use of the vaccine is limited to cats in high-risk areas. Most household cats are at a low risk for infection.

FELINE IMMUNODEFICIENCY VIRUS (FIV): Like human immunodeficiency virus (HIV) in humans, the feline immunodeficiency virus suppresses the immune system. Cats with compromised immune systems are susceptible to a number of illnesses and diseases, including respiratory infections, ear infections, urinary tract infections, and skin infections. After contracting FIV, a cat can live months or years before her immune system is compromised to the point she is chronically ill. Some cats with FIV may enjoy a relatively good quality of life for a long period of time. But because they can still spread this disease to other cats, FIV-infected cats should be kept isolated.

A vaccine is available to prevent FIV, but it has its drawbacks. Cats that have received the vaccine will test positive on the antibody screening tests used to determine if a cat has the disease. It is difficult to tell whether the vaccine or an FIV infection has caused the positive test result. Your veterinarian can advise you if this vaccination is a good option for your particular situation.

EXTERNAL PARASITES

Parasites can compromise your pet's health. It is vitally important to prevent and treat both external and internal infestations. External parasites, which include fleas, ticks and mites, live on or near the cat's skin surface. Internal parasites, such as intestinal worms and heartworms, live within the cat's body.

FLEAS: The flea is an insect that feeds on the blood of mammals. These blood-sucking creatures are notorious for their ability to proliferate—a small flea problem can quickly become a large flea problem, as fleas can quickly spread to all the cats and dogs in a household. After their populations become too dense to survive on the pets, fleas will begin to target humans.

Fleas are especially dangerous to young kittens, as the insects can consume enough blood to cause life-threatening anemia. The bites cause intense itching in animals, which can result in hair loss and skin infections from excessive scratching. Worst of all, fleas serve as intermediate hosts

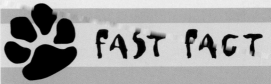

FAST FACT

An adult female flea can produce up to 50 eggs per day.

for tapeworms, which they pass on to pets.

There are several methods for controlling flea infestations in pets. Among the effective and convenient methods for killing and repelling fleas are spot-on treatments, monthly oral applications, and biannual injections. Be sure to purchase products formulated specifically for cats. You should also be vigilant about the products you use on other pets in your household. Some products made for dogs contain permethrin, an insecticide that is toxic to cats. Make sure that all the flea control products you use in your household are safe for felines. If you're not sure, ask your veterinarian for recommendations.

If a flea infestation is especially severe, you may also need to treat your cat's environment. Flea eggs fall onto carpets, along baseboards, and into cat beds. Use a flea control carpet spray or shampoo in these areas. Such products often have a residual effect that prevents infestations for several weeks or months.

External parasites like fleas can make your cat uncomfortable or sick. Prevention is much less expensive than treating a flea-infested house.

Ticks can carry disease, so they should be removed promptly if found on your cat's skin.

Again, make sure the product is labeled as safe for cats.

TICKS: The tick is a small, spider-like creature with a round, flat body. Ticks often live in grassy or wooded areas, where they wait for potential hosts to walk by. After crawling onto animals or humans, they find a suitable place to bury their heads into the skin for a blood meal. Although tick bites are painless, ticks can transmit diseases.

Your cat should take her job of self-grooming seriously enough to keep these pests out of her pristine

You won't be able to see mites, but you may see their effects on your cat—discharge from the ears or patches of mangy fur.

coat. However, at some point she may encounter a tick that is so firmly attached she can't get it off by herself. In this case, you'll have to help her. Take a pair of tweezers and grasp the tick close to the skin and quickly pull it off. Then kill the tick by immersing it in rubbing alcohol. Afterward, use rubbing alcohol to disinfect your hands and the site of the bite.

Many products used to repel fleas also help repel ticks. To prevent infestations, use flea and tick collars or spot-on treatments on your pet. Keep the ticks out of your yard by keeping the grass mowed and moving wood piles to the outskirts of your property. Be aware that indoor-only cats are not immune to encountering these pests. Ticks may enter

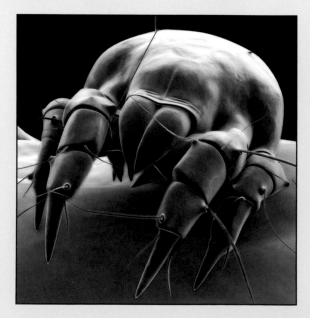

your home on another pet or even on humans, so preventatives are still worth consideration.

MITES: Related to ticks, mites are so small they cannot be seen with the naked eye. But their presence is often evident on a pet suffering from infestation. Mites cause hair loss, skin irritation, and intense itching. The most common ones found on cats are ear mites—infestations result in a dark, gritty discharge from the cat's ears. Because this symptom can also result from an ear infection, have your veterinarian examine the cat to determine if mites are the cause.

Other kinds of mites can also cause problems for the cat. Demodex mites and sarcoptic mites cause a condition called mange. In cats, mange results in patchy hair loss, especially around the head. Demodectic mange is not considered contagious. It results when the cat has a suppressed immune system and can't stop the population growth of demodex mites that normally exist on its skin. Sarcoptic mange, on the

TICKS AND FELINE DISEASE

Babesioisis—Causes chronic symptoms of loss of appetite, weakness, and a rough hair coat appearance. Most cats respond well with antiprotozoal medications.

Cytauxzoonosis—This often fatal disease mostly affects cats in the southeast United States. It causes loss of appetite, listlessness, and fever. Antiprotozoal treatment may be effective.

Ehrlichiosis—Symptoms include loss of appetite, listlessness, fever, and diarrhea. Treatment with tetracycline or other medications is usually effective.

Heamobartonellosis—Symptoms may include anemia, loss of appetite, weakness, and fever. Blood transfusions may be necessary, and treatment with tetracycline medications is usually prescribed.

Tularemia—Also known as rabbit fever, tularemia causes fevers and enlarged lymph nodes in cats. An abscess may develop at the site of the tick bite, and there may be discharge from the nose and eyes. Antibiotics are often used for treatment.

other hand, is a highly contagious condition. When left untreated, both demodectic and sarcoptic forms of mange can progress and affect large portions of the cat's body. When infection has progressed from localized to generalized, it becomes much more difficult to treat.

Cheyletiella mites cause another highly contagious type of mange known as walking dandruff. Infestation causes mild itching, but the most notable symptom is the excessive dandruff in the cat's coat.

Fortunately, most types of mite infestations of cats are uncommon. But in all cases, prompt veterinary attention is very important. Cats typically respond to the irritation caused by these bugs with excessive scratching, which can lead to sores and skin infections.

INTERNAL PARASITES

Internal parasites may live hidden from sight, but they are far from harmless. Like external parasites, they thrive at the expense of your cat's health. Almost all cats are infected with internal parasites at some time in their lives.

Prevention and treatment of these pests should be a part of your cat's regular health care routine. Because not all deworming products are effective against all types of internal parasites, it is important that your veterinarian check your cat's stool sample at each annual visit. Proper identification of the culprit parasites will allow him to prescribe the right treatment.

INTESTINAL WORMS: Intestinal worms find their way into your cat in several different ways. Worm eggs or larvae can be picked up from the soil on your cat's feet. Then the parasites are ingested during the process of grooming. Some worms can be acquired when your cat eats an infected rodent or other animal. Some worm larvae can penetrate the skin to get inside your cat. Tapeworms can be passed on to your pet by infected fleas.

Kittens are especially vulnerable to intestinal worms, which they can acquire through their mother's milk. A bloated belly, lack of energy, and diarrhea are indications that your kitten is carrying a load of unwanted passengers. The small size and immature immune systems of kittens puts them at a particularly high risk of suffering the detrimental effects of these parasites. For these reasons, kittens should receive several worming treatments before the age of six months.

Roundworms are the most common intestinal worms found in cats. These worms can grow to be five inches long. They can easily be passed on to humans, especially children, so it is a good idea to keep them out of your pets.

Hookworms are shorter and thinner than roundworms. They get their name from their hook-like mouths, which they use to anchor themselves to the wall of the intestine as they feed on blood. Although more common in dogs, hookworms still find the cat's intestines to be a hospitable environment. Their eggs, which are shed through the cat's feces, can then infect other animals.

Tapeworms also fasten themselves to the cat's intestinal wall as they

Cats infected with hookworms can transmit these parasites to their owners.

feed and grow. These prodigious parasites can reach several feet in length. Tapeworms have segmented bodies that break off into smaller segments called proglottids, which contain both male and female reproductive organs. These confetti-like segments are excreted with the feces, which ultimately cause further infection. Getting rid of tapeworms involves more than treating the cat with deworming medications—the fleas that transmit tapeworms must also be eradicated.

FELINE HEARTWORM: Once considered a parasite that primarily affected dogs, heartworm can also infect cats. In some cases, the cat's immune system can kill the invading heartworm larvae. But in other cases, the larvae manage to reach the adult worm stage and cause problems. Heartworm disease has symptoms common with other illnesses, such as vomiting, coughing, and difficulty breathing. It is believed that heartworm infection in cats was frequently misdiagnosed in the past.

Heartworm larvae are transmitted by infected mosquitoes. In dogs the larval stage of heartworm migrates to the heart, where it takes up residence, matures, and begins to reproduce. However, in cats the parasite can end up in other parts of the body and

THE DANGER OF HEARTWORMS

Heartworms are a concern for all cat owners. The graphic above illustrates the cycle of heartworm development. When a mosquito (1) bites a cat, it can inject microfilaria into her bloodstream. The microfilaria travel through the bloodstream to the heart (2), where they grow into heartworms (3) and multiply, clogging the cat's heart. If left untreated, heartworms can kill.

causes different kinds of problems. The feline body is not hospitable to heartworms, so these parasites do not reproduce as prolifically or grow as large as they do in canines. However, their effect on feline health can still be deadly, which is why many veteri-narians now recommend regular heartworm prevention for cats.

Typical methods for preventing heartworm involve spot-on treatment or a monthly pill given throughout mosquito season. The preferred treat-ment for cats that have already acquired heartworm disease is to treat the symptoms and allow the cat's system to take care of the worms.

NEUTERING AND SPAYING

Your mixed breed cat has lots and lots of company in the feline world! Pet overpopulation is a serious concern throughout the world, especially for mixed breed cats. Because of the shortage of available homes for them, more mixed breed cats are euthanized each year than any other domestic animal. For this reason alone, you should neuter or spay your pet.

There are other good reasons to neuter or spay your cat. Intact cats tend to have litter box lapses. And when in pursuit of mates or defending their territory, they can caterwaul at all hours of the night. If you want to avoid territorial marking of urine in your home, and if you relish a good night's sleep, make sure your pet is spayed or neutered.

If you think allowing your cat to have a litter of kittens might be fun, you'll be disappointed to find that caring for the newborns is expensive and labor-intensive. If you really love kittens, volunteer to care for and play with all the homeless cats living at your local shelter.

Surgical sterilization should be done by the time your cat is six months old. Although any type of surgery involves some risks, spaying and neutering procedures are performed so frequently that complications and adverse reactions are rare. Cats also tend to recover quite rapidly. Discuss these procedures and the postoperative care thoroughly with your veterinarian.

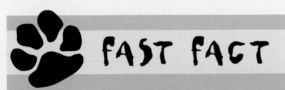

FAST FACT

The beliefs that neutering or spaying a cat will change his or her personality or make the cat fat are myths. Here are some good reasons to neuter or spay your pet:

- Neutered and spayed animals are healthier. They can't suffer health problems related to the reproductive organs.
- Neutering and spaying helps to eliminate undesirable behaviors, like urinating in the house.
- Neutering and spaying prevents unwanted litters of kittens.

DECLAWING AND ALTERNATIVES

Declawing is the surgical removal of a cat's claws. Some pet owners commonly have their cat declawed to prevent damage to their household furnishings. However, over the past two decades, cat owners have become much more enlightened about this procedure. Many people now consider declawing to be cruel and unnecessary. Cats are exceptionally intelligent creatures that are perfectly capable of learning where they can and cannot scratch. The issue, then, is finding the right training technique and deterrents that work so your cat uses her scratching post.

If your cat seems to be having difficulty keeping her paws where you think they belong, don't get frustrated. Many animal welfare organizations offer free professional advice on this topic. Contact your local animal shelter or visit the Cats International Web site. An answer to your problem may be right at your fingertips.

Experienced cat owners quickly learn that they can avoid problems by choosing furnishings that are not "cat magnets." Cats love to scratch on rough, penetrable materials. They are more likely to ignore furniture covered with tightly-woven and smooth fabrics. These types of fabrics also do not get pet hair trapped in the weave so easily.

However, you can't be expected to buy all new furniture just because you got a new cat. If all attempts at training your feline to stop clawing the couch fail, you may consider declawing as a slightly more preferable alternative to relinquishing your cat to the nearest shelter. But be aware that declawed cats must be kept strictly as indoor pets. When outdoors, they won't be able to defend themselves against attacks by other animals. And declawed cats cannot climb trees to escape danger. You will have to take precautions to keep your clawless kitty safe. If you chose to have your cat declawed, be sure to discuss all the risks with your veterinarian.

COMMON HEALTH CONDITIONS

Cats are a hardy species. But even indoor cats, which are not exposed to as many contagious elements as outdoor cats, can get sick occasionally. Common illnesses in cats include upper respiratory infections, heart disease, kidney disease, urinary tract disease, skin conditions, hyperthyroidism, and cancer. Recognizing the

FAST FACT

Does your cat claw in all the wrong places? In order to avoid the needless declawing of cats, the nonprofit educational organization Cats International provides information on how to keep your cat from ruining the furniture. The group guarantees that it can help anyone train any cat to use a scratching post. Check out the Web site www.catsinternational.org for valuable information.

symptoms of these conditions can help you obtain prompt treatment for your cat and increase the chances for a good outcome.

UPPER RESPIRATORY INFECTION: Upper respiratory infections are quite common in cats, especially kittens. The majority of these infections are caused by feline viral rhinotracheitis and feline calicivirus. But respiratory infections can also be caused by other viral agents. Infected cats will appear to have a cold, and exhibit symptoms like sneezing, coughing, and discharge from the eyes and nose.

In mild cases, cats recover on their own. But they should be monitored closely to make sure the condition does not become more serious. Symptoms of profuse nasal or eye discharge, difficulty breathing, or depression are signs that your cat needs to see a vet. Kittens are particularly vulnerable to adverse effects of respiratory illness and should receive quick veterinary attention.

HEART DISEASE: The most common heart condition seen in cats, both mixed breed and pedigreed, is hypertophic cardiomyopathy (HCM). For unknown reasons, it tends to affect primarily male cats. This condition causes a thickening of the heart muscle, which prevents the heart from operating efficiently. Symptoms may

WHEN TO SEEK HELP

Watch for the following signs of illness in your cat and seek prompt veterinary attention:

Behavioral changes	Listlessness
Coughing	Pale gums
Diarrhea	Raised third eyelids
Difficulty breathing	Refusal to eat
Discharge from eyes or nose	Rough coat
Drooling	Skin irritation
Fever	Sneezing
Hair loss	Vomiting
Itching	Weight loss

include a heart murmur, difficulty breathing, or lack of energy. However, in many cases the condition goes undetected until sudden death occurs.

When HCM is detected, the prognosis for an affected cat is good. Although the condition is a progressive disease, it can be managed with medications.

URINARY TRACT DISEASE: Feline lower urinary tract disease (FLUTD) affects the urinary bladder, sphincters, and urethra of cats. There are several different forms of this disease. The ones of most concern to cat owners are those that cause a partial or total obstruction of the urethra. Symptoms of an obstruction include straining to urinate, frequent attempts to urinate,

bloody urine, urinating outside the litter box, and indications of pain or discomfort.

A urinary blockage requires immediate veterinary attention, as it can be fatal. Male cats, which have narrow urethras, are at higher risk than females for suffering this problem. Once affected by this condition, cats have a high incidence of recurrence. Fortunately, you can reduce the chance of recurrence by providing a special diet. If your pet has had FLUTD, your veterinarian can help you implement a plan to manage it.

SKIN CONDITIONS: Many different conditions can compromise the integrity of your cat's skin. Parasites, allergies, fungal infections, and hormonal imbalances can all result in

TALK TO YOUR VET

Topics you may want to discuss with your vet:

- Any problem behaviors you have been experiencing with your cat
- Any unusual behaviors your cat has exhibited
- Any signs or symptoms of illness your cat has displayed

- Neutering or spaying your cat
- Vaccinations your cat may need
- Appropriate diet for your particular cat
- Dental care your cat may need
- Microchipping your cat

hair loss, rashes, redness, scales, dandruff, sores, or infection. To treat skin conditions effectively, you need to get a correct diagnosis from your veterinarian. You can then use the appropriate medications, diet changes, and dietary supplements to improve your cat's skin condition.

HYPERTHYROIDISM: The hormones in the body enable growth, reproduction, and many other functions. They are produced by glands, which make up the endocrine system. The thyroid gland is part of this complex system, and when it doesn't operate properly, serious problems can result. Hyperthyroidism occurs when the thyroid gland becomes enlarged and produces increased levels of hormones.

Symptoms of hyperthyroidism can include weight loss, increased appetite and thirst, disheveled appearance, and behavior changes. Blood tests can confirm the diagnosis. Treatment of hyperthyroidism depends on the severity of the condition and the effect the disease has had on kidney function. Medications or surgery may be recommended.

CANCER: There are many different types of cancer, and the disease affects many different parts of the body. But a diagnosis of cancer doesn't necessarily mean a dire outcome for your pet. Many forms of cancer are now treatable.

During grooming sessions you should evaluate your cat carefully for any symptoms of cancer. Signs may include lumps or growths that increase in size, sores that won't heal, weight loss, and pain or lameness. Check your cat regularly, especially as she grows older. The sooner you seek veterinary attention for cancer, the better the chances for a full recovery.

❧❧❧❧

There are many factors that contribute to a healthy cat—good diet, plenty of exercise, a safe environment, and proactive health care. But there is one thing, above all others, that will predispose your pet to become ill— stress. Cats are known to be at a much higher risk for various health conditions when their feline nerves are frazzled. So while your purring pet provides a form of stress relief for you, be sure to provide a calm stress-free environment for her as well.

CHAPTER SEVEN

Caring for Your Senior Cat

If there's one thing cats can teach us about life, it's how to grow old gracefully. Their strong survival instincts lead them to hide their aches and pains or other weaknesses. Because of this, you need to be exceptionally observant of your senior feline in order to detect any age-related health problems.

HEALTH PROBLEMS

As your venerable feline reaches senior status—over 10 years of age—you may observe that she sleeps a little

---

It is normal for a senior cat to spend more time sleeping than playing. Just like humans, cats slow down as they age.

more than she did in her early years. She also may not have the desire to play as often. And when she does play, she has less stamina. These behaviors are your signal to watch for other signs of aging that may require veterinary attention.

HEARING AND VISION LOSS: Cats tend to adapt quite easily to many consequences of old age, such as the loss of hearing and vision. A reduction in these senses occurs gradually and usually doesn't cause any significant problems for most cats. But if you notice a sudden loss of these abilities, along with any other symptoms such as pain, head shaking, or pawing of the ears, you should take your cat to the vet.

Be patient with your older cat, and keep her hearing or vision deficiencies in mind. If your kitty doesn't come when you call her, it could be because she doesn't hear you. To get her attention, speak loudly or use a noisemaker. Cats can compensate for loss of vision by using their whiskers and the pressure receptors on their feet. But you will help your older cat tremendously if you don't change her environment. Avoid moving furniture and other items around in your home.

ARTHRITIS: If you notice your cat has a slight limp, an arched or stiff back, or a shortened gait, she may have arthritis. This inflammation and stiffness of the joints can be managed with dietary supplements like glucosamine and chondroitin, which can help lubricate the joints and prevent further damage. Pain medications that minimize discomfort are also available.

If your aged cat is overweight, put her on a diet to shed those extra pounds and lessen the stress on her joints. It is worth asking your veterinarian about remedies for arthritis, as proper care can tremendously improve the quality of your senior cat's life.

DENTAL PROBLEMS: Dental issues that were inconspicuous during a cat's younger years can become problems later in life. They may cause infections, pain, and tooth loss in the senior feline. Be sure that your older cat receives veterinary dental exams every six months. Once a tooth is lost, it can't be replaced.

FAST FACT

Never assume your aged cat has to suffer the consequences of age. There are many treatments and products available to assist with age-related health problems. Seek the advice of your veterinarian.

Older cats will experience many changes in the way their bodies function. You will need to watch your pet's behavior more closely as she ages, so that you recognize potential health conditions early. Medical treatment or changes in diet can help your furry friend live longer and more comfortably.

If your elderly cat refuses to eat, shows signs of depression, paws at her mouth, shakes her head, is frequently drooling, or has bad breath, she should be examined for possible dental problems. Your veterinarian may recommend that your cat receive a professional teeth cleaning. This procedure, which involves scraping the teeth clean and polishing them, is performed under anesthesia to prevent your cat from feeling any discomfort.

The importance of good dental health cannot be understated. Periodontal disease, or gum disease, can result in infections that migrate to other parts of the body. Once rooted in other tissues and organs, these infections can become life-threatening.

NUTRITION

The senses of hearing and vision aren't the only functions that tend to wane with age. Internal organs also lose their ability to operate as efficiently. The older cat's digestive system may not be able to absorb some nutrients as readily as it once did. Kidney, liver, and heart functions may diminish. As their bodily processes slow down, older cats have less energy. Such changes may indicate that you need to make nutritional adjustments in your senior cat's diet.

SPECIAL DIETS: There are numerous commercially prepared special diets for cats. However, none of them should be used without veterinary guidance—in fact, most are available only by veterinary prescription. These diets are used to address specific health issues. They should not be used unless you have obtained an accurate veterinary diagnosis. Otherwise, they can do more harm than good.

Still, if your cat appears to be suffering from an age-related condition, you should ask your veterinarian for advice about special diets. An

older cat's changes in digestion may have resulted in chronic constipation or caused problems with hairballs. These problems can be addressed by giving your cat a diet high in fiber. Special diets can also help reduce urinary tract problems or increase the longevity of cats suffering from various kinds of organ failure.

In addition to prescribing a special diet for your cat, your veterinarian may recommend other treatments. Certain vitamins or supplements can ease symptoms of old age, such as poor skin and coat conditions caused by digestive problems. Managing your cat's age-related condition through diet is a great way to help your cat weather the effects of aging.

WEIGHT CONTROL: Most people expect their geriatric cats to gain weight as they age into a more sedentary lifestyle. But the opposite is just as likely to be true. Older cats

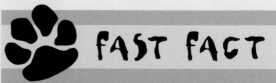

FAST FACT

Because of the cat's small size, any weight loss can quickly become a serious health issue. Monitor your senior cat's weight, and take her to the veterinarian if her weight has noticeably dropped.

can lose their appetite due to a reduced sense of taste or because of other age-related conditions.

There are special diets available to help both overweight and underweight cats. However, if your senior companion is getting a bit obese because she's spending more time lounging than leaping, she would be better off if you simply cut back on her normal portions. Special diets for weight loss typically reduce cer-

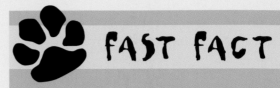

tain nutrients, like fat. That change in diet can have an undesirable effect on your cat's coat quality and energy level. Again, always consult your veterinarian before implementing a special diet.

GROOMING

Is your long-in-the-tooth cat becoming short on personal hygiene? If your veterinarian has given your elderly kitty a clean bill of health, but she still looks unkempt, she may have lost interest in self-grooming. Stretching out on the windowsill for a good doze has probably become a preferred activity.

If this is the case, you may need to help your cat out in the grooming department. A good brushing once or more per week can help your kitty retain a more youthful and clean appearance. You can also purchase grooming products that will persuade your cat to groom herself more frequently. There are some kinds of

Extra weight will place extra stress on your older cat's heart and other organs. Your veterinarian will provide advice on dietary changes you can implement to slim her down.

brushes that cats absolutely love to rub against, especially when the item is dabbed with a little catnip. A well-preened kitty not only looks good; she feels good, too!

EXERCISE

Your senior cat may be slowing down, but it often takes only a little rekindling to awaken the predator within. Just because your cat is past her prime, you have no reason to stop giving her kitty activities to do. Boxes or paper bags to play in, a new toy once in a while, or "find the treat" games can keep your kitty mentally active as well as physically fit throughout her senior years. However, don't stress your aged kitty's joints and overtax her muscles by encouraging high jumps and leaps.

KEEPING COMFORTABLE

It's a privilege to enjoy every phase of your cat's life, even the latter years. You're not done making memories

If you notice that your cat has lost interest in regular grooming, you may have to brush her more often than you did in the past. An older cat will probably appreciate the extra attention.

HELP YOUR SENIOR CAT

Things you can do to help your older cat:

- Switch to a more palatable food if your senior cat shows declining appetite.

- Provide softer foods for a cat that has lost teeth.

- To help with digestion divide meals into smaller portions given at more frequent feedings.

- Provide a litter box with a cut-out doorway or lower sides for ease of entry.

- Do not stress an older cat by bringing a kitten into the home.

- Provide interesting but low-impact toys.

- Provide ramps or arrange furniture so that your cat can reach favorite perches.

- Brush the older cat gently, as her skin gets thinner with age.

together yet. Your older cat can continue to enrich your life. But at her advanced age, it's only fair to give her some special considerations. Spoiling your longtime friend with a few amenities does more than show her how much you appreciate her. It helps you provide her with the best quality of life.

Older cats are more prone to the effects of cold temperatures, so make sure your cat's beds and perches are not located where drafts can chill her. If you really want to put a little more warmth into your senior kitty's life, give her a heated cat pad. This energy-efficient item can be placed on your cat's window perch, under her cat bed, or on her favorite corner of the couch. Be sure to purchase the kind made especially for cats, as regular heating pads can get much too hot.

If your feline is afflicted with arthritis, provide her with a little

FAST FACT

The older cat's more sedentary lifestyle puts little wear on claws. As a result, you typically need to trim the claws more often.

FAST FACT

Forty percent of cats over the age of 16 exhibit signs of disorientation. Such behavior includes wandering around as if lost, crying, or pacing. Sometimes these symptoms are due to a health condition, or they can be caused by cognitive dysfunction syndrome, an age-related memory condition. See your veterinarian for a correct diagnosis and possible treatments.

assistance so she can reach the high perches she enjoys. Cat ramps or steps can help your kitty scale furniture and cat trees comfortably and safely.

SAYING GOODBYE

It's not easy to see a beloved pet suffer at the end of a good life. Then again, it's not easy to make the decision to euthanize your pet, either. But if you observe your cat carefully, she may just make the decision for you.

Has your cat lost the vitality in her eyes? Has her hunter's spirit been extinguished? Does she gaze at you weakly with a gentle wish to be released from life? Some cats communicate very obviously that they are ready to go. Other cats rally for awhile, only to slip back into poor health.

In either case, you will find it hard to accept that it is time to say goodbye. You have spent many years building and nurturing a relationship with this very special creature, and it is never easy to part. However, it's not fair to allow an animal to suffer in order to avoid your inevitable heartache of loss. Your cat trusts you to do the right thing.

EUTHANASIA: The term *euthanasia* means "good death," and it is one of the best gifts you can give a pet whose passing is difficult and prolonged. Your veterinarian can administer drugs that will immediately relax your cat, make her fall into a deep sleep, and help her pass gently from this world without pain.

Afterward, you will be given the choice to cremate or bury your long-time companion. Whichever method of interment you choose, you should feel comfortable with it, as this is one of the ways you cope with your loss.

COPING WITH LOSS: It's difficult to deal with your feelings and intensity of emotions when a beloved pet has died. But there are a number of things you can do to help find a sense of closure.

One of the best ways to cope with a loss is to honor the feline that graced your life. Make a donation in

Reviewing old photos of you and your beloved pet can help ease the pain of loss.

your pet's name to a worthy feline organization or your local animal shelter. Plant a bush or tree in your cat's honor. Create a garden stone as a remembrance. Or put together a photo album that documents the time you shared together.

Try to avoid dwelling on your loss. Pay attention to the loved ones who still share your life. Make plans for a future trip or activity. And most importantly, keep busy. Whether you immerse yourself in work or hobbies, you'll find an occupied mind has little room for sadness.

If you find the loss of your cat to be exceptionally devastating, do not hesitate to seek grief counseling. Your local animal shelter may offer, or be able to refer you to, grief counseling sessions. These programs are designed specifically for those who have suffered the loss of a pet.

ৰ৶৶৶

Cats teach us, challenge us, and most of all, love us. No matter what experiences you have with your particular feline, you are guaranteed to become wiser and richer because of her!

Organizations to Contact

American Animal Hospital Association
12575 West Bayaud Avenue
Lakewood, CO 80228
Phone: 303-986-2800
E-mail: info@aahanet.org
Web site: www.aahanet.org

American Kennel Club
8051 Arco Corporate Drive, Suite 100
Raleigh, NC 27617
Phone: 919-233-9767
Web site: www.akc.org

American Cat Fanciers Association (ACFA)
P.O. Box 1949
Nixa, MO 65714-1949
Phone: 417-725-1530
E-mail: acfa@aol.com
Web site: www.acfacat.com

American Holistic Veterinary Medical Association (AHVMA)
2218 Old Emmorton Road
Bel Air, MD 21015
Phone: 410-569-0795
Fax: 410-569-2346
E-mail: office@ahvma.org
Web site: www.ahvma.org

American Humane Association
63 Inverness Dr. East
Englewood, CO 80112
Phone: 303-792-9900
Fax: 303-792-5333
E-mail: info@americanhumane.org
Web site: www.americanhumane.org

American Society for the Prevention of Cruelty to Animals
424 East 92nd St.
New York, NY 10128
Phone: 212-876-7700
E-mail: information@aspca.org
Web site: www.aspca.org

American Veterinary Medical Assn.
1931 North Meacham Rd., Suite 100
Schaumburg, IL 60173
Phone: 847-925-8070
Fax: 847-925-1329
E-mail: avmainfo@avma.org
Web site: www.avma.org

Canadian Cat Association (CCA)
5045 Orbitor Dr., Bldg. 12, Suite 102
Mississauga, Ontario L4W 4Y4
Canada
Phone: 905-232-3481
Web site: www.cca-afc.com

**Canadian Federation
of Humane Societies**
102-30 Concourse Gate
Ottawa, Ontario, K2E 7V7
Canada
Phone: 613-224-8072
Toll free: 888-678-CFHS
E-mail: info@cfhs.ca
Web site: www.cfhs.ca

**The Canadian
Kennel Club**
89 Skyway Avenue, Suite 100
Etobicoke, ON, M9W 6R4
Canada
Phone: 416-675-5511
Fax: 416-675-6506
E-mail: information@ckc.ca
Web site: www.ckc.ca/en

**Cat Fanciers'
Association (CFA)**
1805 Atlantic Avenue
Manasquan, NJ 08736-0805
Phone: 732-528-9797
E-mail: cfa@cfa.org
Web site: www.cfainc.org

**Cat Fanciers'
Federation (CFF)**
P.O. Box 661
Gratis, OH 45330
Phone: 937-787-9009
E-mail: CFF@siscom.net
Web site: www.cffinc.org

Delta Society
875 124th Avenue NE. Suite 101
Bellevue, WA 98005
Phone: 425-679-5500
E-mail: info@deltasociety.org
Web site: www.deltasociety.org

Humane Society of the U.S.
2100 L St., NW
Washington, D.C. 20037
Phone: 202-452-1100
Fax: 202-778-6132
Web site: www.hsus.org

The International Cat Association
PO Box 2684
Harlingen, TX 78551
Phone: 956-428-8046
E-mail: information@tica.org
Web site: www.tica.org

The Kennel Club of the UK
1-5 Clarges Street
Piccadilly London W1J 8AB
United Kingdom
Phone: 0870 606 6750
Fax: 020 7518 1058
Web site: www.thekennelclub.org.uk

**National Association of
Professional Pet Sitters (NAPPS)**
17000 Commerce Parkway, Suite C
Mt. Laurel, NJ 08054
Phone: 856-439-0824
Web site: www.petsitters.org

**Orthopedic Foundation
for Animals (OFA)**
2300 East Nifong Boulevard
Columbia, MO 65201
Phone: 573-442-0418
Fax: 573-875-5073
E-mail: ofa@offa.org
Web site: www.offa.org

Pet Loss Support Hotline
College of Veterinary Medicine
Cornell University
Ithaca, NY 14853-6401
Phone: 607-253-3932
Web site: www.vet.cornell.edu/public/
    petloss

Pet Sitters International (PSI)
201 East King Street
King, NC 27021
Phone: 336-982-9222
Web site: www.petsit.com

UK National Pet Register
74 North Albert Street, Dept 2
Fleetwood, Lancasterhire
FY7 6BJ
United Kingdom
Web site: www.nationalpetregister.org

Further Reading

Becker, Marty. *The Ultimate Cat Lover: The Best Experts' Advice for a Happy, Healthy Cat with Stories and Photos of Fabulous Felines.* Deerfield, Fla.: HCI Books, 2008.

Eldredge, Debra M. *Cat Owner's Home Veterinary Handbook.* Hoboken, N.J.: Howell Book House, 2008.

Moore, Arden. *The Cat Behavior Answer Book: Practical Insights and Proven Solutions for Your Feline Questions.* North Adams, Mass.: Storey Publishing, 2007.

Moore, Arden. *Happy Cat, Happy You: Quick Tips for Building a Bond with Your Feline Friend.* North Adams, Mass.: Storey Publishing, 2008.

Palika, Liz. *The Ultimate Pet Food Guide: Everything You Need to Know About Feeding Your Dog or Cat.* Cambridge, Mass.: Da Capo Press, 2008.

Pryor, Karen. *Clicker Training for Cats.* Waltham, Mass.: Sunshine Books, 2003.

Rainbolt, Dusty. *Cat Wrangling Made Easy: Maintaining Peace and Sanity in Your Multicat Home.* Guilford, Conn.: The Lyons Press, 2007.

Shojai, Amy D. *Complete Care for Your Aging Cat.* New York: NAL Trade, 2003.

Internet Resources

http://www.aspca.org/pet-care/poison-control

Not sure what plants are poisonous to your cat? The ASPCA Animal Poison Control Center provides a list of toxic plants along with photos to help you identify poisonous hazards.

http://catagility.com

The Web site for the International Cat Agility Tournaments can give you a peek at this new and fun feline sport.

http://catnet.stanford.edu/articles/enclosures.html

Stanford Cat Network Web page provides links to various sites offering ideas and plans for outdoor cat enclosures.

http://www.catsinternational.org

The information on the Cats International Web site can help you find solutions to common feline behavioral issues. Don't get frustrated—get answers!

http://www.funcatnames.com

Naming your new cat is fun! It's also permanent, so make sure you pick the right moniker. This Fun Cat Names Web site can help you choose a name that fits.

http://www.petfinder.com

This nationwide database can help you locate adoption agencies and adoptable cats in your geographical area. It also features classified ads for pets that need new homes.

http://www.petsitters.org

This Web site helps match pet owners with experienced pet sitters in their area.

Index

Numbers in **bold italics** refer to captions.

Contributors

Pet writer and author **Janice Biniok** has written numerous books and articles on companion animals, including *The Poodle* (Eldorado Ink, 2008) and *The Yorkshire Terrier* (Eldorado Ink, 2008). She is a member of the Cat Writers' Association and the Dog Writers Association of America. Janice lives on a small farm in Waukesha, Wisconsin, with her husband, two sons, and several four-legged members of the family. You can learn more about her at www.TheAnimalPen.com.

Senior Consulting Editor **Gary Korsgaard, DVM,** has had a long and distinguished career in veterinary medicine. After graduating from The Ohio State University's College of Veterinary Medicine in 1963, he spent two years as a captain in the Veterinary Corps of the U.S. Army. During that time he attended the Walter Reed Army Institute of Research and became Chief of the Veterinary Division for the Sixth Army Medical Laboratory at the Presidio, San Francisco.

In 1968 Dr. Korsgaard founded the Monte Vista Veterinary Hospital in Concord, California, where he practiced for 32 years as a small animal veterinarian. He is a past president of the Contra Costa Veterinary Association, and was one of the founding members of the Contra Costa Veterinary Emergency Clinic, serving as president and board member of that hospital for nearly 30 years.

Dr. Korsgaard retired in 2000. He enjoys golf, hiking, international travel, and spending time with his wife Susan and their three children and four grandchildren.